# IN BRIEF

BY JUDITH KITCHEN

NONFICTION

*Only the Dance: Essays on Time and Memory*

*Understanding William Stafford*

*In Short: A Collection of Brief Creative Nonfiction*
(co-editor with Mary Paumier Jones)


POEMS

*Perennials*

Since this page cannot legibly accommodate all the copyright notices,
pages 286–88 constitute an extension of the copyright page.

The text of this book is composed in Adobe Garamond
Desktop composition by Thomas O. Ernst


Library of Congress Cataloging-in-Publication Data

In brief : short takes on the personal / edited by Judith Kitchen
and Mary Paumier Jones.
p.   cm.
ISBN 0-393-31907-5   (pbk.)
ISBN 978-0-393-31907-1  (pbk.)
1. American essays—20th century. 2. Autobiographies.
I. Kitchen, Judith. II. Jones, Mary Paumier.
PS688.I48  1999
814.5408—dc21
98-51869
CIP

W. W. Norton & Company, Inc.
500 Fifth Avenue, New York, N.Y. 10110
www.wwnorton.com


W. W. Norton & Company Ltd.
15 Carlisle Street, London W1D 3BS


3  4  5  6  7  8  9

# IN BRIEF

Short Takes on

the Personal

■

Edited by

Judith Kitchen

and Mary Paumier Jones

W. W. Norton & Company ■ New York ■ London

DEDICATION

For our daughters-in-law, Robin and Liz.

Our thanks again to our husbands, Stan and Jim Edd, and our sons, William, Matthew, Morgan, and Tyler, for their continuing love and support. Thanks also to our indefatigable editor, Carol Houck Smith. And finally, our thanks to all the fine writers gathered here. We hope you enjoy each other.

# Contents

# INTRODUCTION

A few years ago, as avid readers of nonfiction, we noticed a new trend toward brevity. Not only were ever shorter pieces being published, but longer essays, we noticed, could be made up of shorter sections in a "mosaic" style. We began gathering short pieces (under 2,000 words) that could stand on their own. Such a "short," we concluded, could range from fragment to finished essay, anecdote to memoir, description to commentary. It could be a story, a meditation, a speculation, an hypothesis. The result was our 1996 anthology, *In Short: A Collection of Brief Creative Nonfiction.*

In the years since, the form has proliferated. Personal writing has become even more diverse. New magazines such as *Doubletake* are featuring short pieces in every issue; *Seneca Review* has recently added a section on the "lyric essay"; best-selling memoirs (such as those by James Salter and Vivian

Gornick) have popularized the mosaic style. The memoir has come of age—and in some ways seems to define our age. Readers are hungry for the language of human, humane minds at work.

For our second collaboration, we chose to concentrate on these recent developments in nonfiction. *In Brief* offers a variety of new tastes. Once again brevity was a main concern, but so was the quality of personal reflection and speculation. The authors here are young and old, established and emerging (including first publications), from many walks of life and every section of the country. What they have in common is the power of the personal—a single voice conveying individual experience.

The personal goes beyond the simple first-person retelling of a story or anecdote. The personal is a way of seeing the world, of examining its meanings, of exploring and expressing an interior life. It is intimate without being maudlin. It is private without being secret. It allows the reader into the heart and mind of the writer, connecting us to each other.

The personal gives new energy to traditional points of view. Most of these pieces do rely on a first-person narrator, but the emphasis is on *person*. The voices are brilliantly varied. They range from Frank McCourt's conversational style to William Maxwell's meditations on the nature of growing old, from Anne Panning's rapid-fire reconstruction of her parents' lives to Mary Oliver's lyric description of a littered beach, accented by her distinctive diction (sometimes nothing is more personal than an adjective). Josephine Jacobsen moves readily from "I" to "we," in the end speaking for the way her experience applies to all of us. Some writers resort to the second-person "you" to generalize and make universal their individual experience, asking the reader to *participate* in the event rather than simply observe it. For a few, the distance of the third person is what allows the self to come into focus. And some, like Andre Dubus, imagine the lives of others while locked in their own very real circumstances—in his case, a wheelchair. Whether it's by the first person "I" of most of these pieces, the direct address employed by James Alan McPherson, or a detailed third-person account like that of Kelly Cunnane, the reader is brought into an intimate space defined by the voice and perspective of the author.

Woven throughout this collection are some surprising coincidental subjects (cattle, wedding dresses, radios, Cape Canaveral, the smell of a grandmother's garden) as well as some familiar threads: women's lives, travel, aging parents, loss, religion, lies, disillusionment, letters, technology, landscape, and, above all (see the pivotal essay of Kathleen Dean Moore), *language*. We have orchestrated some pieces that resonate with one another into "strings." For example, "A Sense of Water" moves inevitably toward its counterpart, "A Sense of Wonder." A sequence on women's lives reveals the importance of food in how we hold families together. A series on the art of lying alerts us to both its creative and its destructive sides. Many essays speak to each other across the pages of the collection—all those "difficult daughters," those men in their cars—reinforcing an idea or adding a new dimension.

*In Brief* includes openings (Brady Udall and Dermot Healy), middles (Frank McCourt and Mary Clearman Blew), and endings (Edwidge Danticat and William Kloefkorn) taken from longer works. Lyrical moments are excerpted for their own vivid color (James Salter's paean to flying), or a life's story is compressed to barely a page (Jeanne Brinkman Grinnan's tribute to her father). We looked for a combination of length, depth, and wholeness. For the most part, we looked for work from writers we had not anthologized before, but we've also included some writers who, we feel, have come to define the short form—Stuart Dybek, Bernard Cooper, Jane Brox, Kathleen Norris—and some we discovered through NPR broadcasts, prose poems, eulogies, even e-mail. In each case, we've looked for the voiceprint, the defining vision, that marks the piece as personal.

Another thing these pieces have in common is the belief that there is a real world—and that we live in it. This may seem obvious, but the years between *In Short* and *In Brief* have seen a burgeoning not only of creative nonfiction but also of academic theorizing about it. The result has been much talk about how, because truth is subjective, it doesn't matter if you make things up—even in nonfiction. We buy the first part: truth is subjective and, by definition, there is nothing we are more subjective about than our own lives. But we do not buy the specious logic of the conclusion. If a writer calls a piece *nonfiction*, there is an implied contract with the reader: "This is factual as best I can remember and re-create it."

Good nonfiction writers do more, of course. They let the reader know that their "take" on events is an individual one. The same material, even the same life experience, can be viewed in multiple ways. Frank McCourt, for example, makes us see through a boy's eyes, feel his father's situation, and understand his mother's helpless anxiety—all in one passage. And Ariel Dorfman reminds us of the broad political spectrum against which any memoir is set.

Sandwiched between Harriet Doerr's personal memoir and Josephine Jacobsen's more abstract reverie on the nature of memory, *In Brief* presents the reflections and musings of writers who think about what it is to live in these times and recall what it was to live in other times. They take us on journeys across the country and into their most intimate thoughts. We experience what it is to come of age and what it is to grow older. From the "green" of Marjorie Sandor's rhapsody to new love to the "dark emerald" of M. J. Iuppa's grief, the collection gives glimpses into the ways we think and act and into the ways experience can be shaped in language that is fresh and inventive.

If these short pieces employ many techniques of fiction—narrative, dialogue, descriptive imagery, point of view, interior voice, etc.—they do so not to invent imaginary worlds (what Charles Baxter refers to as "the parallel universe of literature") but to make something *of* the facts. We have been picky about this to the point of checking with the writer when a piece felt "stranger than truth." Robert Shapard went so far as to send us a copy of a photo of the grandmother in question (as Columbia on a float in a 1918 Armistice Day parade) and said that the "the incident and circumstances did happen and have always seemed vivid to me." Conversely, we asked the author of a novel if a striking short chapter wasn't really nonfiction. Seamus Deane assured us it was. When W. Scott Olsen describes a landscape "107 miles west of Fargo," we expect to be able to verify that the land is indeed flat as you drive west through that part of North Dakota. And when Jonathan Raban relates being in a storm in eastern Montana, we trust his particular version of rain.

Nonfiction writers often admit that the places where they were tempted to invent can, if they stick with the scrupulously factual, end up yielding the deepest genuine insight and best writing. Creative nonfiction works in a space of its own. Neither documentary nor fiction, it invites us to speculate, but always about the world we know, have known, or could know. How a piece is narrated gives it its flavor. Jamaica Kincaid's article on gardening becomes an extended metaphor for the process of writing. Kinereth Gensler discovers metaphor in her journeys at sea. Albert Goldbarth lends his quirky wit and unique passion to the making of a minyan.

Castle Freeman, Jr. indulges in a leisurely speculation about strangers. And Jane Brox contemplates the meanings of bread. In each case, the subject matter is nonfiction; the writing makes it literary, or creative. Imagination becomes a way to probe reality. The real world we are lucky enough to live in is revealed as endlessly rich and deep.

JUDITH KITCHEN
MARY PAUMIER JONES

# IN BRIEF

HARRIET DOERR

## Low Tide at Four

What I remember of those summers at the beach is that every afternoon there was a low tide at four.

I am wrong, of course. Memory has outstripped reality. But before me as I write, in all its original colors, is a scene I painted and framed and now, almost fifty years later, bring to light.

Here, then, is a California beach in summer, with children, surfers, fishermen, and gulls. The children are seven and three. We are on the sand, a whole family—father, mother, a boy and a girl. The year is 1939. It is noon. There will be a low tide at four.

Days at the beach are all the same. It is hard to tell one from another. We walk down from our house on the side of the hill and stop on the bluff to count the fishermen (five) on the pier and the surfers (three), riding the swells, waiting for their waves. We turn into Mrs. Tustin's pergola restaurant for hamburgers. Though we recognize them as the best in the world, we never eat them under the matted honeysuckle of the pergola. Instead, we carry them, along with towels, buckets, shovels, books, and an umbrella, down the perilous, tilting wooden stairs to the beach. Later we go back to the pergola for chocolate and vanilla cones.

"Ice cream special, cherry mint ripple," says Mrs. Tustin on this particular day, and we watch a fat man lick a scoop of it from his cone. We wait for him to say, "Not bad," or "I'll try anything once," but he has no comment. A long freight train rattles by on the tracks behind the pergola. As we turn away, Mrs. Tustin says, "The world's in big trouble," and the fat man says, "You can say that again. How about that paperhanger, Adolf?" But it's hard to hear because of the train.

Back on the beach, our heads under the umbrella, we lie at compass points like a four-pointed star. The sun hangs hot and high. Small gusts of wind lift the children's corn-straw hair. We taste salt. Face down, arms wide, we cling to the revolving earth.

Now Mr. Bray, the station agent, a middle-aged Mercury in a shiny suit, crosses the dry sand in his brown oxford shoes. He is delivering a telegram. Everyone listens while I read the message from our best and oldest friends. Sorry, they can't come next weekend after all. Good, we say to ourselves, without shame.

I invite Mr. Bray to join us under the umbrella. "Can't you stay on the beach for a while?" He pauses with sand sifting into his shoes. Oh, no, he has to get back to his trains. He left his wife in charge, and the new diesel streamliner will be coming through.

At this moment a single-seated fighter plane from the navy base north of us bursts into sight along the shore, flying so low it has to climb to miss the pier. The children jump into the air and wave. The pilot, who looks too young for his job, waves back.

"Look at that," says Mr. Bray. "He could get himself killed."

Time and the afternoon are running out. A fisherman reels in a corbina. Three gulls ride the swells under the pier. The children, streaked with wet sand, dig a series of parallel and intersecting trenches into the ebb tide. Their father walks to the end of the pier, dives into a swell, rides in on a wave, and walks out to the end of the pier again. I swim and come back to my towel to read. I swim and read again.

*Winesburg, Ohio; Sister Carrie; Absalom, Absalom!; Ethan Frome; The Magic Mountain; Studs Lonigan; A Handful of Dust; A Room with a View.* There are never books enough or days enough to read them.

I look up from my page. Here is old Mrs. Winfield's car being parked at the top of the bluff. It must be almost four. Her combination driver, gardener, and general manager, Tom Yoshimura, helps her into a canvas chair he has set up in front of the view. His wife, Hatsu, new from Japan, is stringing beans for dinner in Mrs. Winfield's shingled house on the hill. Hatsu can't speak English. She bows good morning and good afternoon.

Mrs. Winfield has survived everything: her husband's death and the death of a child, earthquakes, floods, and fires, surgical operations and dental work, the accidents and occasional arrests of her grandchildren. All these, as well as intervals of a joy so intense it can no longer be remembered. I watch Tom Yoshimura bring her an ice cream cone from the pergola.

It is four o'clock. We are standing in shallow water at low tide. The children dig with their toes and let the waves wash in and out over their feet. They are sinking deeper and deeper. During the summer, their skins have turned every shade of honey: wildflower, orange, buckwheat, clover. Now they are sage. I look into my husband's face. He reaches over their heads to touch my arm.

At this time on this August day in 1939, I call up my interior reserves and gather strength from my blood and bones. Exerting the full force of my will, I command the earth to leave off circling long enough to hold up the sun, hold back the wave. Long enough for me to paint and frame low tide.

MARJORIE SANDOR

# Rhapsody in Green

A few years ago, when I was married and living uneasily
in Florida, I believed that there was, in a town twelve miles
away, a little restaurant with green upholstery—a certain
green—that served the best breakfast. This restaurant,
which I thought existed at a bend in the road near some
railroad tracks, had that sheerly impossible quality we sometimes ascribe to material things—often to restaurants,
sometimes to whole cities we can't seem to get back to. If we
could only get there again, we think, our lives would be
saved, or a deep, nagging mystery solved at last. Surely
you've heard people go on this way, rhapsodically, about an
armchair they sat in once on a Thursday when they were
twelve, or about the smell of sausage in an English pub on a
rainy day in March 1957. Some apparently trivial things
appear to contain the sublime, and there's no explaining

this to anyone—nor any getting over it. Even Proust wore out his friends, trying.

Still, in my mind's eye was that bend in the road, the railroad tracks, and the breakfast house of my dreams. I drove to the town one day, with a friend who puts up with such eccentricities, and found no restaurant there at all, of course, though I'd gotten the bend in the road right, and the railroad tracks.

"Maybe you dreamed it," said my friend warily.

"Maybe," I said, trying to tamp down the little fear that's been with me since childhood—a fear that, though I seem to get along okay in the world, I'm secretly mad as a hatter.

Then I moved out to the West. And sure enough, that particular shade of green, though not the restaurant, was everywhere: a green somewhere between duck-egg and a Granny Smith apple—only denser, richer, a color never found in nature. Sometimes I'd find it in the mud porch of a turn-of-the-century farmhouse, or on the wall of a new friend's bathroom. It had been there all along, in the paintings of Kandinsky and Chagall, and on the occasional umbrella. It was on a T-shirt I wore until I stained it on the day I ate the best oyster of my life and fell in love when I shouldn't have.

This green is not military, not forest-service. Nor is it the color of small imported Spanish olives or the giant ones stuffed with garlic, though God knows I love olives. Their green has its own pleasures, akin to those of oysters—shiny, subtle harbingers of the primitive—which is why, the day I fell in love when I shouldn't have, I asked for three in my martini. At the time I wondered why the waiter seemed taken aback; the request seemed perfectly natural, no big deal.

We must go beyond, or away from, olives. My green is the color of old walls in photographs of French country houses, of the floors and even the vats of a tortilla factory in Puerta

Vallarta three months before I fell in love when I shouldn't have. It is a color you cannot find in the narrow color strips they give away in paint stores, where the delusional come searching, aching, for the shade of green they've been waiting for all their lives. Chalky, dusky, somewhere between mint and the color of 1950s tile in the kitchen of the house my husband and I bought.

The owner of the paint store looked grieved, as if I'd asked him if there really was a God. "I can't help you," he said mournfully. "That green doesn't exist except in pictures."

Of course not. It can't be found outside, this green—not exactly, though it wants to be, in a way that haunts the edges of almost knowing. It has nothing to do with gardens or gardening, a hobby I'd taken up when my husband and I moved out West—not because I wanted to but because the house we bought had a garden so beautiful it would have been criminal to mow it down. But our garden wasn't that green. Not the green of pear tree leaves nor the green of the rhododendron; not even the greeny-gray of certain aromatic sages that can make you weep for a smell lost from childhood; not even the triple dark green of a trout stream under cloud cover. Here again, however, oysters and olives come to mind—along with that feeling of succumbing to something that laps away at the safe edges of your life, although I refused to fall in love anywhere near that trout stream. I was thirty-six and living in Florida when I fell in love with green, but forty and in another state entirely the day I fell in love when I shouldn't have.

I've asked a psychologist if there is a connection between unmanageable desire and a dream of a green restaurant. She laughed but did not explain her laughter. Is this part of treatment?

Just before I left Florida, I took my friend who puts up with such eccentricities to a tiny inland town under a canopy of oaks and kudzu where a hundred psychics lived and worked. We had made no appointment, but a bulletin board in the town's general store announced the telephone number of the day's psychic "on call." So it came to pass that a woman named Eunice told me what I already knew: that I was "leaving the state," as she put it, "and damn glad to be"; that I would not miss it one bit.

Then she went on. She said she saw me with my hands in the dirt, and she didn't mean that metaphorically. "You're going to be a gardener," she said.

"Not possible," I said. "I don't garden. Not interested."

"Your work will take a turn toward the metaphysical."

"God forbid," I said. "I don't even know what that means."

"You will be lucky in love," she said. "But it won't look like luck for a long time."

We sat a moment in silence.

"Go," she said. "I see a long journey." And then she laughed, and sent me out into her yard, into dazzling uncertainty.

# Late July, 4:40 A.M.

Plains of western Kansas. Across the pavement, a wheat field now stubble is still giving off the earth smells of night. Miles distant, oncoming headlights from an occasional car or truck flare against a background of dusk. Though the sun's first glint over the horizon is a good half-hour away, that eastern rim is already orange, modulating to indigo overhead—with two or three stars so very faint, I'm not sure the growing light hasn't already dissolved them.

On three sides of the "Kountry Korner Grocery/ Restaurant & Truck Stop" a herd of big rigs, some fifteen or twenty, pulses and throbs, motors idling under empty cabs while their drivers order the biscuit and gravy special, or maybe plain eggs, hash browns, and coffee. Walking among those mumbling diesels toward my car, I hear a very American possibility, one we can't remember not having,

can't imagine being without: the road's ongoing promise—
endless, auspicious.

In terms of waste, of pollution, we know a better way
could be found. Just as surely as the bulk and chuff of each
mastodon eighteen-wheeler feels already outmoded, we're certain a better way *will*. Because it must. Yet how could we fail
to be expressions of what we grew up in? A U. S. of cheap
cars, cheap gas, and roads going every which where. Haven't
they made us a people most at home when making good time?
Whipping past dinky towns like dull habits discarded.

Despite that pack of engines idly burning off foliage of the
Carboniferous period, the early air is astonishingly clear, even
delicious. In the waning dusk along I-70's westbound lane,
headlights from the occasional onrushing trucker reflect off a
green-and-white sign placing Salinas and Abilene straight
ahead, Colorado beyond them. It's my way, too. Out of
Illinois for a thousand miles and more, mountains and desert
become my favorite directions. With dawn at my back, a full
moon low in the west, well rested, undersides of the eyelids
not grainy with fatigue, I ride the adrenaline rush of early
hour highway euphoria.

County after county my pickup pours me into a phantasmagoria of phallic silos, ditches where sunflowers flutter like
windmills, fields of hay bales rounded like Iroquois lodges. Far
below the easy equilibrium of high hawks, the plain rolls as if bur-
rowed by some great, loam-shouldering mole. Sioux place names
appear—"Ogallala," for instance. "Oh, Ogallala! Ogallala, oh!"
I pronounce aloud and laughingly often. Over miles of inter-
state, "Ogallala" insists on its syllables: a chant, a sing-song, a
mantra.

Oncoming billboards loom, growing in size like impera-
tives: THREE MILES FROM THE LARGEST PRAIRIE DOG IN THE
WORLD. Stuffed or alive, such a creature abides my visit to

Rexford, Kansas. Which is the more peculiar specimen, I ask myself, that prairie dog or any animal called *Homo Sapiens* who pulls over to see it? Then farther on, 20 MILES TO 5-LEGGED COW, residence unspecified, yet those miles pour past in no time.

With neither need nor intention to stop, I feel motion itself becoming my truest urge. Motion as essence, as life's very definition. Don't we say "animated" of things that move on their own? Of even drawn lines colored for romping across a movie screen. *Anima*, which we've borrowed to say "animal." *Anima*, which in Latin means "soul"—a gift we confer on the road through connotations in "highway," and which that highway returns by seeming to proffer us, its fastest, traveling vertebrates, more future than anybody can have. Diesel cab after cab, all chrome-glint and smoke, rushes toward and past like an explosion. Going west along with me, great double-trailer rigs high as the Wall of China sway slowly as they over-take my speeding six-cylinder truck. Animation: the soul of all highways? Road itself the Prime Mover?

Kansas dwindles, thins to its own state line, then is gone, as into Colorado I hurtle, scattering crows convened by a damp splat of fur-bearing roadkill. Soon, against a background of pine boards once painted but weathered now to a barnwood blue-gray, and in faded red or black lettering, hints at quite a story leap from billboard to billboard, with only a sort of medi-tation space in between: 8 YEARS OF STARVATION HAVE BEEN HARD TO ENDURE. Then a half-mile farther, BETTER TIMES ARE COMING. Another half-mile. MOM DID LET SOME GROW UP TO BE COWBOYS. And another. BEING STARVED ON MY OWN LAND BY MY OWN GOVERNMENT. And another. PRIVATE PROPERTY OR BUREAUCRATIC DICTATORSHIP. Yet another. FROM PRODUCTIVE CITIZEN TO BEGGAR THANKS TO BUREAUCRATS. And so on, to KING BUREAUCRAT VS. CONSTITUTION—thence to—ONE YEAR

SINCE KING'S ORDER: "THESE SIGNS MUST BE REMOVED"—till finally, like a return to some opening F-minor chord—8 YEARS COLORADO STARVATION RANCH.

Beyond and behind that lettering, what's the sad upshot? Beats me. To learn more, I'd have to turn aside, wouldn't I, seek out that rancher or one of his neighbors. Impossible. The road's motion won't let me. "On," it says. "Farther." As for Colorado Starvation Ranch, slow adversity can occur only if we stop, settle down. Which is something the road never does.

JONATHAN RABAN

# Gulleywasher

I loaded two armfuls of books into the boot of the car and headed south to Baker, where I put up in a motel room furnished with junk from the wilder reaches of the 1950s. The pictures on its walls were all of water: two horseback explorers were in the act of discovering a mountain lake; a packhorse bridge spanned a river in what looked like Constable country; printed on dark blue velvet, a Japanese sea was in the grip of a *tsunami*. They were pictures for a dry country. At $23.50 for three beds, a bathroom and a fully equipped kitchen, the room was pleasingly in character with the frugal spirit of the place.

That evening a lightning-storm moved in on Baker from the west. One could see it coming for an hour before it hit: the distant artillery flashes on a sky of deep episcopal purple. As the storm advanced, I sat in a bar on Main Street, reading the life of Patrick Henry in *Four American Patriots: A Book for Young Americans* by Alma Holman Burton.

> 'Colonel Washington,' said Mr. Davies, 'is only twenty-three years old. I cannot but hope that Providence has preserved the youth in so signal a manner for some important service to his country.'
>
> 'Oh,' thought Patrick, 'George Washington has done so much for his country, and he is only twenty-three.'

The people in the bar were huddled and talkative: living by day in so much space and solitude, they evidently liked to squash up close at night. At the back of the place, two poker tables were in session with the players gossiping unprofessionally between reckless bids of 50¢ a time. The slogan in scabbed paint on the bar door announced, *Liquor Up Front, Poker in the Rear.*

> He looked down at his hands. They were brown and rough with toil.
>
> 'Alas!' he said, 'I do my best, and yet I cannot even make a living on my little farm!'
>
> This was quite true.
>
> Patrick could not make his crops grow. Then his house caught fire and burned to the ground. It was all very discouraging!

The snippets of bar conversation were, on the whole, more interesting than Alma Holman Burton's prose. A Mexican seated at the table next to me was talking to a scrawny, pencil-moustached, thirtyish type, perched on a swivel-stool at the bar. The Mexican said he was up in Baker from Wilmer, Texas.

*"Wilmer?"* said the guy at the bar, in a whoop of delighted

recognition. "I know Wilmer! I was in jail in Wilmer. Buy you a drink, man?"

And so, at the age of twenty-three, Patrick Henry, with a wife and little children to provide for, did not have a shilling in his pocket. But his father helped a little and Sarah's father helped a little, and they managed to keep the wolf from the door . . .

. . . which would not have been a dead metaphor to a child in eastern Montana, where wolves picked off the sheep at nights and "wolfers" trapped the animals for bounty.

The thunder was directly overhead, and it was immediately followed by a long kettle-drum tattoo of rain on the roof. The bar went quiet. Everyone in it listened to the rain.

"It's a gulleywasher," the bartender said, gathering in the empties.

The thunder rolled away eastwards, towards North Dakota, but the rain kept coming.

"It's a gulleywasher," said the man who'd done jail-time in Wilmer, as if he had just minted the expression.

A crowd formed at the open doorway of the bar to watch the downpour. The rain fell in gleaming rods. Main Street was a tumbling river, already out of its banks and spilling over onto the sidewalk. Its greasy waters were colored red, white, and blue by the neon signs in the bar window. A truck sloshed past at crawling speed, throwing up a wake that broke against the doors of darkened stores.

"That," said a turnip-faced old brute in a Stetson, speaking in the voice of long and hard experience, "is a gulleywasher."

People craned to see. A couple had brought their toddler along (this was an easygoing bar in an easygoing town); the man lifted her on to his shoulders to give her a grandstand view of the wonder. The rain made everyone young: people dropped their guard in its presence, and the pleasure in their faces was as empty of self-consciousness as that of the toddler, who bounced against her father's neck, saying, "Water. Water. Water." Some shook their heads slowly from side to side, their faces possessed by the same aimless smile. Some whistled softly through their teeth. A woman laughed; a low cigarette-stoked laugh that sounded uncannily like the hiss and crackle of the rain itself.

It went on raining. It was still raining when I drove back to the motel, where the forecourt was awash and the kitchen carpet blackly sodden. I sat up listening to it; attuned now to what I ought to hear. When rain falls in these parts, in what used to be known as the Great American Desert, it falls with the weight of an astonishing gift. It falls like money.

JOHN T. PRICE

# Good Workers

To work, my grandfather said, was to work. To play was to play. And he meant to *work*—digging ditches, shoveling shit for pennies until the flesh on your hands peeled back in red strips. When I was just a teen he told me about those bloody hands with a serious, unfeeling pride that seemed awesome to me, a boy in school, the son of a lawyer.

When I was even younger, maybe four, my grandfather would drive me down to the Gas and Electric Service Garage where he worked, and while there he would let me honk the horns on all the bright yellow company trucks. The way I remember it, it is always winter, and my grandfather picks me up around dusk when the horizon holds a strip of azure beneath the blackness. A few strings of Christmas lights, red and green, linger on this house or that. The cabin of my grandfather's truck is warm, and the crunching snow sounds

cold beneath the deep treads of the tires. In the freezing, concrete yard outside of the Service Garage I see a couple of
slouching figures in army-green parkas. They stand there, next
to the wire fence, leaning slowly to one side then the other,
faceless, breathing cold mist, concerned about something,
somewhere. They are, I am told by my grandfather, *the workers*. Once inside the Garage I see more hulked shadows of
men, all wearing dark gray slacks and grimy white oxfords
with the sleeves rolled up, all standing around in the dry heat,
in the honeyed, whiskey-colored light. I want to remember
that all of them had a slight limp, and that they were picking
the calluses off of their fingers. They gaze at me briefly, emo-
tionless, then continue working or talking or laughing. "Good
men," my grandfather says. "They work hard."

Before long my grandfather grabs me under the armpits
and lifts me into the dark cabby of one of the trucks. He slams
the door, I grasp the wheel and savor the oily, leather smell of
the interior—a big-man smell. I put on the yellow hard-hat.
Slowly at first, then spastically, I press the center of the wheel,
and fill the huge garage with a trumpet-call to announce my
own arrival to work. Ten or fifteen trucks later I'm ready to go,
and so is my grandfather. In his truck, on the way home, I
play with the snaky seatbelt strap, growl like a demon, and
wonder why he sucks on lemon rinds.

Of course he was a drinker—many of them were who
worked with the trucks. At least I remember it that way. A
man, say his name is Carl, has just come in from working on
the trucks that are parked out in the sub-zero Iowa winter. His
heavy black boots are limping snow across the gray floor of the
Service Garage. Because his left leg is shorter than his right, he
has to wear an elevated sole; a sole that catches snow and dirt,
and makes an irregular scraping noise on the cement like a
man rubbing his own stubble. You are a young boy, say, honk-

ing horns, when you see him coming. As he passes, you slouch down in the seat of the truck to hide, because, along with the limp, you notice that the southern border of his gray flattop nearly touches the dark ridge of his eyebrows. He seems, to you, otherworldly. He's cussing through his large lips, something about how this is the goddamned last time he'll work on that carburetor. The *goddamned* last time. Then you see him in the fluorescence of the square breakroom, beneath the dusty 7-Up clock, taking his greasy hide gloves off one finger at a time, reaching into the pocket of his parka for his father's flask, and letting his prominent lower lip lead his mouth to the rim. He'll work a hard, cold afternoon and past supper, making up, perhaps, for being what his older brother in Chicago calls a stupid boozer. Such a man did work there, several such men, and my grandfather told me their stories. They were, at times, a burden to employ, he said, all that guilt and anger built up inside of them. And, of course, there was the drinking. But they were hard workers. Good men.

But the story my grandfather never told was his own—he left that to others. My mother remembers that once, when she was just a young girl, she saw him collapse on the front porch stairs, drunk, and that she screamed because she thought he had polio like her grandma and that he would die. But he was never a violent drunk, she might add. She describes him as a happy, sidewalk-whistler type, a man willing to play jacks with her and her girlfriends on sunny evenings in spite of all the many hours he put in at the Garage. Just like so, on the verge of spilling forth her anger, she thinks of her father's work, his very hard work, and it will soften that anger. The belief that a man who works hard can erase all his sins runs deep into the folds of my family, and, I suspect, into the midwestern landscape in which we were all raised.

By the time I understood the redemptive power of work, I

was three months away from high school graduation, on the cusp of independence, and speculating, as high school seniors often do, that my future would hold nothing but failure and sin. Then, during one evening that March, without prompting, I called Mr. Decker, the owner of a local truck line, and asked him if I could have a job washing trucks, nothing better. He told me to just punch in, anytime.

So I showed up at Decker Truck Line the next Saturday around nine, wearing my father's old work boots, the ones he wore when he shoveled by-products at the Hormel Plant; a job that, as he proudly recalls, left bleeding sores on his hands. I punched in and walked through the huge garage, tracking in snow and dirt, nodding hello to all the mechanics and drivers, breathing cold mist. I walked up a few cement steps into a small, darker garage where the walls smelled mossy, and the long rubber hoses lay around like dead bull snakes on Highway 20, brown and flat and wet. I grabbed two cream-colored buckets, filled them with hot water from the rusty water spout, and added a squeeze or two of soap.

In memory I see my silhouette, dark against the bright light in the open garage door, boyishly thin, kneeling while the steam from the buckets warms my face from the March morning. In that pose I'm feeling, somewhere near the small of my back, that I have arrived, finally, to work. Did I recall, at that quiet moment, all those men, all those workers that haunted the winters of my childhood? Did the soapsuds in the buckets smell like so many old lemon rinds, sucked dry and scattered on the front seat of my grandfather's truck? However it really was then, I see this now: I am scrubbing the trucks furiously, washing the grime from the white metal, pausing to watch it slide down, slowly, in a gray stream, over the tires, along the cement, and, finally, into the drain as if it carries along with it all my future transgressions.

B R A D Y   U D A L L

# One Liar's Beginnings

Before all else, let me make my confession: I am a liar. For me, admitting to being a liar is just about the most difficult confession I could make; as a rule, liars don't like to admit to anything. But I'm trying to figure out how I came to be this way—what influences, what decisions at what forked roads have led me to be the devious soul I am today. And as any clergyman worth a nickel can tell you, before you can discover the truth about yourself, first you must confess.

I can't say I remember the first lie I ever told. It's been so long, and there have been so many lies in between. But I can only believe that my first steps, first day of school, first kiss—all those many firsts we love to get so nostalgic about—none of them was in any way as momentous as that first lie I ever told.

It's a dusty summer day. I am three years old, and in the Udall household there is going to be hell to pay; some fool has

gone and eaten all the cinnamon red-hots my mother was
going to use to decorate cupcakes for a funeral luncheon.

Down in the basement, I am bumping the back of my
head against the cushion of the couch. This peculiar habit,
*head-bouncing* we called it in our house, was something I liked
to do whenever I was nervous or bored. I was most satisfied
with the world when I could sit on that couch and bounce my
head against the back cushion—you know, really get up a
good rhythm, maybe a little Woody Woodpecker on the
TV—and not have anyone bother me about it. Along with
worrying that their son might be retarded on some level, my
parents also became concerned about the living room couch—
all this manic head-bouncing of mine was wearing a considerable divot in the middle cushion (my preferred section) right
down to the foam. So my father, after trying all he could think
of to get me to desist, finally threw up his hands and went to
the town dump and came back with a prehistoric shaggy
brown couch that smelled like coconut suntan oil. He put it
down in the basement, out of sight of friends and neighbors,
and I was allowed to head-bounce away to my heart's content.

So there I am down on the couch, really going at it, while
my mother stomps around up above. She is looking for the
red-hots thief, and she is furious. My mother is beautiful,
ever-smiling and refined, but when she is angry she could
strike fear into the heart of a werewolf.

As for me, I am thoroughly terrified, though not too terrified to enjoy the last of the red-hots. I put them in my mouth
and keep them there until they turn into a warm, red syrup
that I roll around on my tongue.

My mother is yelling out all the kids' names: *Travis!
Symonie! Brady! Cord!* But none of us is dumb enough to
answer. Finally, she stomps down the steps and sees me there
on my couch, bobbing back and forth like the peg on a

metronome, trying not to look her way, hoping that if I can keep my eyes off her long enough she just might disappear.

"Brady, did you eat those red-hots?" she asks, her mouth set hard. I begin to bounce harder.

"Hmmm?" I say.

"Did you eat them?"

I imagine for a second what my punishment will be—maybe spending the rest of the afternoon cooped up in my room, maybe being forced to watch while the rest of the family hogs down the leftover cupcakes after dinner—or maybe she will have mercy on me and opt for a simple swat on the butt with a spatula.

"Did you eat them?"

I don't really think about it, don't even know where it comes from—I look my mother straight in the eye, say it loud and clear as you please: "No."

She doesn't press me, just takes my answer for what it is. Why would she suspect anything from me, a baby who's never lied before, innocent as can be, a sweet little angel who doesn't know any better than to spend all his free time banging his head against the back cushion of a couch from the dump.

"All right," she says, smiling just a little now. She can't help herself—I am that innocent and cute. "Why don't you come upstairs and have a cupcake?"

Right then I stop bouncing altogether. It feels as if there is light blooming in my head, filling me up, giving me a sensation I've never had before, a feeling of potency and possibility and dominion. With a word as simple as "no" I can make things different altogether; no, it wasn't me who ate those red-hots; no, it's not me who deserves a swat on the butt or no cartoons for the rest of the afternoon. What I deserve is a cupcake.

It's a wonderful epiphany: with a lie I can change reality; with a lie I can change the world.

DERMOT HEALY

# from *The Bend for Home*

The doctor strolls into the bedroom and taps my mother's stomach.

You're not ready yet, ma'am, he says to her.

Be the holy, she trustingly replies.

That woman of yours will be some hours yet, he tells my father on the porch. He studies the low Finea sky. You'll find me in Fitz's.

The doctor throws his brown satchel into the back of the Ford that's parked at an angle to our gate and ambles up to the pub. My father sits on a chair at the bottom of the bed. My mother has a slight crossing of the eye, and because she hasn't her glasses on she looks the more vulnerable. He has had water boiling downstairs all day. He's wearing the trousers of the Garda uniform and smoking John Players. The November night goes on. Some time later she goes into labour again. My father runs up the village and gets the doctor from the pub.

He feels her stomach, counts the intervals between the heaves, then says, Move over.

My mother does. He unlaces his shoes and gets in beside her.

Call me, ma'am, when you're ready, he says and falls into a drunken sleep.

My father is waiting impatiently outside on the stairs. Time passes. The snores carry to him. Eventually he turns the handle and peers into the low-ceilinged room. He can't believe his eyes.

Jack, she whispers, get Mary Sheridan, do.

He brings Mary Sheridan back on the bar of his bike. The tillylamps flare. At three in the morning the midwife delivers the child. Where the doctor was during these proceedings I don't know. As for the child, it did not grow up to be me, although till recently I believed this was how I was born. Family stories were told so often that I always thought I was there. In fact, all this took place in a neighbour's house up the road, and it was my mother, not Mary Sheridan, arrived on her bike to lend a hand.

It's in a neighbour's house fiction begins.

SEAMUS DEANE

# Accident, June 1948

One day I saw a boy from Blucher Street killed by a reversing lorry. He was standing at the rear wheel, ready to jump on the back when the lorry moved off. But the driver reversed suddenly, and the boy went under the wheel as the men at the street corner turned round and began shouting and running. It was too late. He lay there in the darkness under the truck, with his arm spread out and blood creeping out on all sides. The lorry driver collapsed, and the boy's mother appeared and looked and looked and then suddenly sat down as people came to stand in front of her and hide the awful sight.

I was standing on the parapet wall above Meenan's Park, only twenty yards away, and I could see the police car coming up the road from the barracks at the far end. Two policemen got out, and one of them bent down and looked under the lorry. He stood up and pushed his cap back on his head and rubbed his hands on his thighs. I think he felt sick. His distress reached me, airborne, like a smell; in a small vertigo, I sat down on the wall. The lorry seemed to lurch again. The second policeman had a notebook in his hand and he went round to each of the men who had been standing at the corner when it happened. They all turned their backs on him. Then the ambulance came.

For months, I kept seeing the lorry reversing, and Rory Hannaway's arm going out as he was wound under. Somebody told me that one of the policemen had vomited on the other side of the lorry. I felt the vertigo again on hearing this and, with it, pity for the man. But this seemed wrong; everyone hated the police, told us to stay away from them, that they were a bad lot. So I said nothing, especially as I felt scarcely anything for Rory's mother or the lorry driver, both of whom I knew. No more than a year later, when we were hiding from police in a corn field after they had interrupted us chopping down a tree for the annual bonfire on the fifteenth of August, the Feast of the Assumption, Danny Green told me in detail how young Hannaway had been run over by a police car which had not even stopped. "Bastards," he said, shining the blade of his axe with wet grass. I tightened the hauling rope round my waist and said nothing; somehow this allayed the subtle sense of treachery I had felt from the start. As a result, I began to feel then a real sorrow for Rory's mother and for the driver who had never worked since. The yellow-green corn whistled as the police car slid past on the road below. It was dark before we brought the tree in, combing the back lanes clean with its nervous branches.

FRANK McCOURT

# from *Angela's Ashes*

Grandpa in the North sends a telegram money order for five pounds for the baby Alphie. Mam wants to cash it but she can't go far from the bed. Dad says he'll cash it at the post office. She tells Malachy and me to go with him. He cashes it and tells us, All right, boys, go home and tell your mother I'll be home in a few minutes.

Malachy says, Dad, you're not to go to the pub. Mam said you're to bring home the money. You're not to drink the pint.

Now, now, son. Go home to your mother.

Dad, give us the money. That money is for the baby.

Now, Francis, don't be a bad boy. Do what your father tells you.

He walks away from us and into South's pub.

Mam is sitting by the fireplace with Alphie in her arms. She shakes her head. He went to the pub, didn't he?

He did.

I want ye to go back down to that pub and read him out of it. I want ye to stand in the middle of the pub and tell every man your father is drinking the money for the baby. Ye are to tell the world there isn't a scrap of food in this house, not a lump of coal to start the fire, not a drop of milk for the baby's bottle.

We walk through the streets and Malachy practices his speech at the top of his voice, Dad, Dad, that five pounds is for the new baby. That's not for the drink. The child is above in the bed bawling and roaring for his milk and you're drinking the pint.

He's gone from South's pub. Malachy still wants to stand and make his speech but I tell him we have to hurry and look in other pubs before Dad drinks the whole five pounds. We can't find him in other pubs either. He knows Mam would come for him or send us and there are so many pubs at this end of Limerick and beyond we could be looking for a month. We have to tell Mam there's no sign of him and she tells us we're pure useless. Oh, Jesus, I wish I had my strength and I'd search every pub in Limerick. I'd tear the mouth out of his head, so I would. Go on, go back down and try all the pubs around the railway station and try Naughton's fish and chip shop.

I have to go by myself because Malachy has the runs and can't stray far from the bucket. I search all the pubs on Parnell Street and around. I look into the snugs where the women drink and in all the men's lavatories. I'm hungry but I'm afraid to go home till I find my father. He's not in Naughton's fish and chip shop but there's a drunken man asleep at a table in the corner and his fish and chips are on the floor in their *Limerick Leader* wrapping and if I don't get them the cat will so I shove them under my jersey and I'm out the door and up the street to sit on the steps at the railway station eat my fish and chips watch the drunken soldiers pass by with the girls that giggle thank the drunken man in my mind for drowning the fish and chips in vinegar and smothering them in salt and then remember that if I die tonight I'm in a state of sin for stealing and I could go straight to hell stuffed with fish and chips but it's Saturday and if the priests are still in the confession boxes I can clear my soul after my feed.

The Dominican church is just up Glentworth Street.

Bless me, Father, for I have sinned, it's a fortnight since my last confession. I tell him the usual sins and then, I stole fish and chips from a drunken man.

Why, my child?

I was hungry, Father.

And why were you hungry?

There was nothing in my belly, Father.

He says nothing and even though it's dark I know he's shaking his head. My dear child, why can't you go home and ask your mother for something?

Because she sent me out looking for my father in the pubs, Father, and I couldn't find him and she hasn't a scrap in the house because he's drinking the five pounds Grandpa sent from the North for the new baby and she's raging by the fire because I can't find my father.

I wonder if this priest is asleep because he's very quiet till he says, My child, I sit here. I hear the sins of the poor. I assign the penance. I bestow absolution. I should be on my knees washing their feet. Do you understand me, my child?

I tell him I do but I don't.

Go home, child. Pray for me.

No penance, Father?

No, my child.

I stole the fish and chips. I'm doomed.

You're forgiven. Go. Pray for me.

He blesses me in Latin, talks to himself in English and I wonder what I did to him.

I wish I could find my father so I could say to Mam, Here he is and he has three pounds left in his pocket. I'm not hungry now so I can go up one side of O'Connell Street and down the other and search pubs on the side streets and there he is in Gleeson's how could I miss him with his singing,

*'Tis alone my concern if the grandest surprise*
*Would be shining at me out of somebody's eyes.*
*'Tis my private affair what my feelings would be*
*While the Green Glens of Antrim were welcoming me.*

My heart is banging away in my chest and I don't know what to do because I know I'm raging inside like my mother by the fire and all I can think of doing is running in and giving him a good kick in the leg and running out again but I don't because we have the mornings by the fire when he tells me about Cuchulain and DeValera and Roosevelt and if he's there drunk and buying pints with the baby's money he has that look in his eyes Eugene had when he searched for Oliver and I might as well go home and tell my mother a lie that I never saw him couldn't find him.

I know I don't have to tell Mam anything, that soon when the pubs close he'll be home singing and offering us a penny to die for Ireland and it will be different now because it's bad enough to drink the dole or the wages but a man that drinks the money for a new baby is gone beyond the beyonds as my mother would say.

ANNE PANNING

# Remembering, I Was Not There

I t is 1963. My mother, Barbara Louise Griep, works at the family creamery, sells buckets of ice cream and bricks of butter, saves wages for the wedding. She has already purchased yards and yards of creamy white satin and made, by herself, one hundred cloth-covered buttons to go down the back. She sits home nights with pins held between her teeth: stitch and hem. Her older sisters wash dishes and laugh; her mother, my grandmother Lucille, is not happy with the engagement, and says so. My mother's soon-to-be-husband, Lowell William Arthur Panning, is out driving country roads, crushing and tossing empty beer cans out the window of his light blue '57 Chevy Custom.

Do not marry him, I wish to warn her. He's wild already, though oddly charming with his square black glasses, his white T-shirt, his loose rolled-up jeans. His hair rolls back at the forehead like an Elvis or better, a Buddy Holly with narrow boy's hips, the beginning of pockmarks.

I would stop them surely, but this: *impossible.* They cannot hear me. I am born two whole years later, the first baby daughter with black hair like an Indian's, cloudy gray eyes that would magically turn gold years later. There is already the first son, James, with black piercing eyes from the start. We will thrill them, James and I, blinking, innocent, adorable bundles. My mother will give up The School of Nursing. She will give up delicate white hose and the starched white caps with pointed wings she has so dreamed of wearing.

I wish to sit them both down, say *don't.* You will destroy yourselves, everything dear. You will make your lives harder than they have to be.

My father, Lowell W. A. Panning, is finishing up his studies at Lee's Barber College on 7th Street in St. Paul. He learns about scalp diseases, shaving with a straightedge, crew cuts, dandruff, and proper placement of comb and scissors in the hands. A barber? Just months ago he was almost a professional baseball player with the Milwaukee Braves, the Chicago Cubs, the Minnesota Twins. The scouts were there with clipboards, Lowell W. A. Panning was on the mound, bases were loaded, and he struck the batter out—other fantastic feats. The scouts buzzed with offers, shook the nimble hands of my father that would become so adept at haircuts mere months later.

So close.

The next weekend my father was caught with vodka and beer, kicked off the team: the end, but *almost.* This is the story of his life—*almost*—and he will tell me this tale of near-fame and glory repeatedly as I get older, as I learn of his many defeats. He will tell the story belching over a six-pack at age forty-one.

The day before the wedding, my father's grandfather dies. This is the William Arthur of my father's namesake. He has a long sober face from generations of no touch, no hugs in the Panning family. He dies from lack of affection and love—a dry, curled-up gray heart. My mother and father call each other up on the phone: what do we do, what do we do about the wedding? It is too late to cancel or postpone. Both know it.

That night, my mother goes to sleep in the north bedroom for the last time, feet curled up in her nightgown. The room is painted soft yellow, and shadows of maple leaves move across the wall like waving hands: good-bye. She places her palms together and presses them under the pillow; she's eighteen. She has been a good girl her whole life. She wonders if her Lowell W. A. Panning is sad about the death. She, herself, feels no sadness. She worries; she convinces herself this is what people do: marry. She knows she will change him; he will be better. And herself? She puts herself on hold, stops, to become a wife.

My father is out on the farm, on the porch, listening to the creak of the old windmill. Beer flows. His sparkling bachelorhood wavers in front of him. He contemplates kissing all the fun that is his life good-bye for a wife. His father, my grandfather Wilbert, cuffs him on the head, untucks his soiled undershirt, and sighs. "This is about booze," my grandfather says, fat and angry. "Dammit. You have to take care of that girl." He goes inside.

My father loves her. He thinks she is a prize. Plus, he has been waiting for her to finish high school so they can finally do it, marry. His only gripe is the wedding day falls on pheasant hunting opener. In a secret way he cannot explain, he would rather be out with his shotgun.

He hopes he can be a good barber, provider. How can I tell him he will do so well at one but not the other?

When my mother walks down the papered aisle, it crunches. I am in the shadows, tiny and invisible, marveling at her golden hair, her long slender back, her dark brown eyes that are fixed steadily on the cross in front of her. I am the little girl she will someday tell, "I have never got anything I have wanted, Anne. Do you know how that feels? Nothing. Be careful with marriage." Even though she is not.

I will cause her my own share of grief later, but on their wedding day, when Minnesota winds blow cool and the church bell rings, I watch her in wonder and alarm, my hands up over my open mouth. *Help. Don't.* I watch her in fear, scared for myself.

The honeymoon is a no-big-deal. They drive up to a motel in Ham Lake with no television and no swimming pool. It is not even two hours away from the town they both grew up in. The sun on my mother's head makes her warm and sleepy. My father rubs her cheek with a knuckle as a semi-truck passes. My mother holds her shiny diamond up in the air and wiggles her fingers. The glitter alerts me to the new anti-life that is forming—one minus one equals zero. I see figures of them both melting into a black hole I might fall into. I see my mother fascinated by her new wifeness, and shudder. My father stops at the store for a twelve-pack. Just in case we get thirsty, he says, but fools neither of them.

Still 1963, and already a Panning's Barber Shop. John Kennedy is shot, and my father swoons into Reggie's Bar next door. The ceramic barber's chair is left pumped up high, spinning. It is dark in the bar and my father is crying. He doesn't know why, but I could tell him. I could tell him it is not being loved and touched as a child, a cold mother and cold father and little food for so many years—lost youth. These are his problems, I could tell him, but don't.

My mother is at home, sewing brass buttons onto her hand-knit cardigan. The television is on, but she is not surprised. She has enough sense to know anyone that good, that groomed, is bound to die in office. She doesn't cry, but lets out a long, dry wail and is fine. She needs a friend. Everyone is gone. She has given up her life. She irons, reads, cleans, gets ready to have a baby. What is a national tragedy to her when she has already lost it all?

When I do finally spring to life, after James, there are only three of us at home: boy, girl, mom. I learn to think of father as absent, invisible. I learn to take care of my mother, who is really just a girl. I learn to be quiet so she doesn't yell. At age four, I tell my mother that I can get a job so there is more money. At age six, I learn to walk in my shoes carefully so they don't wear out. I learn to misunderstand men at age ten when I see James getting a BB gun when there is supposedly no money for me to join Junior Great Books Club.

My father sails in and out. He dances drunk and lets James and me hang on his flexed biceps when he's in the mood. Take a picture of me and the kids like this! he shouts at my mother, then throws up. And my mother . . . my mother. I see it happening, I know it will happen, I try to warn her. She does not leave him when everything screams *leave*. She's in it for the kids, she tries to believe and stand by. I am unfortunately old enough to grasp it all.

Before I was born, I knew this would happen.

ANNE CARSON

# Very Narrow

*Water is best.*
  —PINDAR

*Memory is of the past.*
  —ARISTOTLE

*No that's not her.*
  —MY FATHER

Surely the world is full of simple truths that can be obtained by asking clear questions and noting the answers. "Who is that woman?" I overheard my father ask my mother one night when I was coming down the stairs to the kitchen. It took me a moment to realize he was asking about me—not because I did not know by then that he was losing his mind, which was obvious in other ways, but because he used the word *woman*.

I was not "woman" to him. I stopped halfway down the

stairs. It reminded me of a night when I was twelve or thirteen. Coming down the same stairs, I heard him in the
kitchen talking to my mother. "Oh, she won't be like them,"
he was saying with a sort of glow in his voice. It was the last
time I heard that glow. Because soon afterward I did, to my
dismay, begin to be like them—as the Chinese proverb says,
"There was blood in the water trough early one morning."

I am not a person who feels easy talking about blood or
desire. I rarely used the word *woman* myself. But such things
are the natural facts of what we are, I suppose we have to follow out these signs in the endless struggle against forgetting.
The truth is, I lived out my adolescence mainly in default of
my father's favor. But I perceived that I could trouble him less
if I had no gender. Anger tired him so. I made my body as
hard and flat as the armor of Athena. No secrets under my
skin, no telltale drops on the threshold. And eventually I
found—a discovery due, in fact, to the austerities of pilgrim-
age—that I could suppress the natural facts of "woman" altogether. I did so. Unfortunately by then his mind was too far
gone to care.

I lived alone for a long time.

What happened to me after that takes the form of a love
story, not so different from other love stories, except better
documented. Love is, as you know, a harrowing event. I
believed in taking an anthropological approach to that.

Even now it is hard to admit how love knocked me over. I
had lived a life protected from all surprise, now suddenly I was
a wheel running downhill, a light thrown against a wall, paper
blown flat in the ditch. I was outside my own language and
customs. Why, the first time he came to my house he walked
straight into the back room and came out and said, "You have
a very narrow bed." Just like that! I had to laugh. I hardly
knew him. I wanted to say, Where I come from, people don't

talk about beds, except children's or sickbeds. But I didn't. Humans in love are terrible. You see them come hungering at one another like prehistoric wolves, you see something struggling for life in between them like a root or a soul and it flares for a moment, then they smash it. The difference between them smashes the bones out. So delicate the bones. "Yes, it is very narrow," I said. And just at that moment, I felt something running down the inside of my leg. I had not bled for thirteen years.

Love is a story that tells itself—fortunately. I don't like romance and have no talent for lyrical outpourings—yet I found myself during the days of my love affair filling many notebooks with data. There was something I had to explain to myself. I traveled into it like a foreign country, noted its behaviors, transcribed its idioms, prowled like an anthropologist for the rare and unwary use of a kinship term. But kinship itself jumped like a frog leg, then lay silent. I found the kinship between a man and a woman can be a steep, whole, excellent thing and full of languages. Yet it may have no speech. Does that make sense?

One night—it was the first winter my father began to have trouble with his mind—I was sitting at the kitchen table wrapping Christmas presents. I saw him coming down the stairs very slowly, holding his hands in front of him. In his hands were language and speech, decoupled, and when he started to talk, they dropped and ran all over the floor like a bag of bell clappers. "What happened to you to I who to? There was a deer. That's not what I. How many were? No. How? What did you do with the things you dripped no not dripped how? You had an account and one flew off. That's not. No? I. No. How? How?" He sat down all of a sudden on the bottom step and turned his eyes on me, clearly having no idea in the world who I was, or how he came to be there with me, or what should happen next. I never saw a human being so naked. His face the face of a fledgling bird, in what fringe of infant evening leaves, in what untouched terror lapped.

Sometimes you come to an edge that just breaks off.

The man who named my narrow bed was a quiet person, but he had good questions. "I suppose you do love me, in your way," I said to him one night close to dawn when we lay on the narrow bed. "And how else should I love you—in your way?" he asked. I am still thinking about that.

Man is this and woman is that, men do this and women do different things, woman wants one thing and man wants something else and nobody down the centuries appears to understand how this should work. "Every day he'd come in from the fields and throw his old filthy hat on my clean tablecloth that we're going to eat off—sweatband down!" says my mother, still furious, and he's been gone how long? years now.

JEANNE BRINKMAN GRINNAN

# Adjustments

It is the last Sunday in October. Time to set the clocks back to eastern standard time, a task my father always took upon himself. Fussing with the clocks. Fine-tuning them, making them accurate.

My mother stands on a chair, reaching out precariously to wind the clock. I stand next to her, fearful that she'll fall. I know that her do-it-herself nature is two-edged. Why just last week, the wheels on the garbage tote got away from her, pulling her down. She fell, bruising both knees badly. I wish that my worry could protect her in some way.

My mother winds the clock. It is another of the "firsts" we encounter since the death of my father in August. Marking his birthday, changing the oil in the car, closing the cottage for another season. It is a strange lens through which I now view the world. To find my father missing in the happenings of every day.

As she turns the key, rewinding the spring mechanism, my mother says, "I had quite a time this morning, adjusting the clocks." I nod sadly, recognizing yet another way we experience his loss.

I think about my father and his meticulous attention to detail. Of the pleasure he found in carving small birds out of basswood or constructing outriggers and sailboats from kits we gave him for Christmas. Last week I came across an old shoebox on the sun porch. It contained the components of a paper clock he had been constructing.

Years ago he discovered a radio station that aired a special broadcast every Saturday. Precisely at noon a signal was sent from the Royal Observatory in Greenwich, England, the site of the prime meridian. My father would synchronize his watch—and my mother's—with the place that marked the origin of time. On those Saturdays, I believe my father tried to lasso time—to cast a net around it and offer it to my mother—a thing distilled and pure.

The *prime meridian*! Words that encompass ancient notions, describing the indescribable, defining the nature of things taken on faith. Words that, as a child, cast a spell over me, naming a place where meaning could stand still: proclaiming an absolute where everything was held in perfect balance.

My mother stands on a chair. Turning the hands backward as if we could relive that hour, do it over again.

WILLIAM MAXWELL

# Nearing 90

Out of the corner of my eye I see my ninetieth birthday approaching. It is one year and six months away. How long after that will I be the person I am now?

I don't yet need a cane but I have a feeling that my table manners have deteriorated. My posture is what you'd expect of someone addicted to sitting in front of a typewriter, but it was always that way. "Stand up straight," my father would say. "You're all bent over like an old man." It didn't bother me then and it doesn't now, though I agree that an erect carriage is a pleasure to see, in someone of any age.

I have regrets but there are not very many of them and, fortunately, I forget what they are. I forget names too, but it is not yet serious. What I am trying to remember and can't, quite often my wife will remember. And vice versa. She is in and out during the day but I know she will be home when evening comes, and so I am never lonely. Long ago, a neighbor in the country, looking at our flower garden, said, "Children and roses reflect their care." This is true of the very old as well.

I am not—I think I am not—afraid of dying. When I was seventeen I worked on a farm in southern Wisconsin, near Portage. It was no ordinary farm and not much serious farming was done there, but it had the look of a place that had been lived in, and loved, for a good long time. The farm had come down in that family through several generations, to a woman who was so alive that everything and everybody seemed to revolve around her personality. She lived well into her nineties and then one day told her oldest daughter that she didn't want to live anymore, that she was tired. This remark reconciled me to my own inevitable extinction. I could believe that enough is enough.

Because I actively enjoy sleeping, dreams, the unexplainable dialogues that take place in my head as I am drifting off, all that, I tell myself that lying down to an afternoon nap that goes on and on through eternity is not something to be concerned about. What spoils this pleasant fancy is the recollection that when people are dead they don't read books. This I find unbearable. No Tolstoy, no Chekhov, no Elizabeth Bowen, no Keats, no Rilke. One might as well be—

Before I am ready to call it quits I would like to reread every book I have ever deeply enjoyed, beginning with Jane Austen and going through shelf after shelf of the bookcases, until I arrive at the "Autobiographies" of William Butler Yeats. As it is, I read a great deal of the time. I am harder to please, though. I see flaws in masterpieces. Conrad indulging in rhetoric when he would do better to get on with it. I would read all day long and well into the night if there were no other claims on my time. Appointments with doctors, with the dentist. The monthly bank statement. Income tax returns. And because I don't want to turn into a monster, people. Afternoon tea with X, dinner with the Ys. Our social life would be a good deal more active than it is if more than half of those I care about hadn't passed over to the other side.

I did not wholly escape that amnesia that overtakes children around the age of six but I carried along with me more of my childhood than, I think, most people do. Once, after dinner, my father hitched up the horse and took my mother and me for a sleigh ride. The winter stars were very bright. The sleigh bells made a lovely sound. I was bundled up to the nose, between my father and mother, where nothing, not even the cold, could get at me. The very perfection of happiness.

At something like the same age, I went for a ride, again with my father and mother, on a riverboat at Havana, Illinois. It was a side-wheeler and the decks were screened, I suppose as protection against the mosquitoes. Across eight decades the name of the steamboat comes back to me—the *Eastland*—bringing with it the context of disaster. A year later, at the dock in Chicago, too many of the passengers crowded on one side, waving good-bye, and it rolled over and sank. Trapped by the screens everywhere, a great many people lost their lives. The fact that I had been on this very steamboat, that I had escaped from a watery grave, I continued to remember all through my childhood.

I have liked remembering almost as much as I have liked living. But now it is different, I have to be careful. I can ruin a night's sleep by suddenly, in the dark, thinking about some particular time in my life. Before I can stop myself it is as if I had driven a mine shaft down through layers and layers of the past and must explore, relive, remember, reconsider, until daylight delivers me.

I have not forgotten the pleasure, when our children were

very young, of hoisting them onto my shoulders when their legs gave out. Of reading to them at bedtime. Of studying their beautiful faces. But that was more than thirty years ago. I admire the way that, as adults, they have taken hold of life, and I am glad that they are not materialistic, but there is little or nothing I can do for them at this point, except write a little fable to put in their Christmas stocking.

"Are you writing?" people ask—out of politeness, undoubtedly. And I say, "Nothing very much." The truth but not the whole truth—which is that I seem to have lost touch with the place that stories and novels come from. I have no idea why. I still like making sentences.

Every now and then, in my waking moments, and especially when I am in the country, I stand and look hard at everything.

ARIEL DORFMAN

# Dealing with the Discovery of Death Inside an Embassy in October of 1973, in Santiago de Chile

So here I am, when all is said and done, in this building that most of the people, peasants and workers whose lives I have sworn to join, here I am in this embassy that most of those people do not even imagine exists, here I am on this piece of territory that is legally considered Argentina, here I am, returned to the protection of the country where I was born, caught in the vicious, saving circle of my origin, here I am with no place to go but back to Buenos Aires.

I know my escape is justified, I know that there was no alternative, but I feel demeaned here, with the innumerable other refugees who have fled to this embassy, I have been stripped naked by the fear that I share with them, humiliated for all the world to see, suddenly homeless, my commitment to the revolution less important than my love of life.

It is here that I meet, face-to-face, the first torture victims of my life. During the last weeks, the rumors have reached me, they say that . . . , you know what they're doing in the Estadio, have you heard what happened to . . . but it was all hear this and hear that and hearsay. Now, a few hours after I manage to be smuggled into the embassy, they are there, these men who have been laid out on a table, stripped naked, not metaphorically as I have, but in the cold reality of a room that smells of piss and vomit and sweat, and their genitals have been connected to a clamp and a hand has pulled a switch, and they are fortunate to have escaped that room and find themselves here, shivering in the sweet October sun of Chile, shivering under a blanket, staring into nothingness, their lips twitching, trying to smile back at me, at anybody who approaches, cringing suddenly, crying out in their nights as we all try to sleep in an air thick with the breathing and the farts and the sighs of almost a thousand people laid out side by side in the great ballroom of the embassy, where only a month ago tuxedoed men leaned forward to murmur compliments to women in long, shuffling dresses, where one of the fugitives himself, Allende's Secretary of the Treasury, sipped a cocktail next to this very piano under which he now tosses and turns, trying to get some rest.

I do not have a blanket. By the time I arrived, it was too late: they had all been handed out to the over nine hundred people who had rushed here before me, and the sadistic chargé d'affaires of the embassy, a tall, flint-eyed man called Neumann, whom we all suspect of Nazi sympathies, has informed the refugees that there is no item in the budget to cover additional blankets. So a friend, known as El Gitano, shares his with me. He is a singer and for the last two years in all our gatherings we have belted out his most famous song. *"Ha llegado aquel famoso tiempo de vivir"*—It's come, that much-awaited time for living—and now that his song has proven to be less a prophecy than a wish, he keeps me warm at night with half his blanket.

I like not having a blanket. It tells everyone that I did not dash to this embassy, it hints to those who came before me that for a few weeks I had stupidly and perhaps even courageously tried to get myself killed.

My unshielded existence is a way of warding off the guilt of having survived, a way of dealing with my decision to go into exile which will remain with me for many, many years, which will really disappear the day fourteen years from now when, with my eight-year-old son Joaquín, I am arrested at the airport in Santiago and deported, when with that violence done to me I can finally, masochistically, feel that I have paid my dues. But here in this embassy it's a way of hurting myself because the Junta hasn't hurt me enough, hasn't hurt me as it is hurting those who remain on the outside of this sanctuary.

I am not to be left in this state of blanketless distinction for long. Some days after I arrive, I am walking in the large garden enjoying the afternoon sun. I have been told to stay away from the eight-foot walls that surround us, but I cannot help it. I am fascinated by the proximity of Chile, just outside, the bustle of the city which I cannot see from here but which I can hear, the sudden singsong conversation of a child and his mother, the throttle of a *micro* changing gears, a man who sharpens knives trundling his cart there on the streets of Santiago, calling out his services.

Suddenly a bundle falls at my feet. For a moment I can't tell where it comes from, but now I see two hands grip the top of the wall—only the fingers, whitened with the effort. Somebody is trying to climb over the wall into the embassy! But now two shots ring out and—no scream, no shout, not even a grunt—just a sort of dull thud on the other side. The police have just killed the man. Why did I imagine it was a man, why have I never pictured a woman? Why did I think he had been killed and not merely wounded or simply stopped in his tracks by the shots? I am cut off from that world out there, at the mercy of my imagination.

In the bundle I find a blanket and a sleeping bag. No passport, no identification papers, nothing to let me know who has offered me these gifts. Because they are gifts. The tragedy of this victim will mean warmer nights for me—and less lonely days, because I will turn the blanket, Linus-like, into an inseparable companion. Whenever I picture myself roaming those halls where Argentine diplomats had hosted the national and international glitterati, I automatically see the blanket of the failed seeker of asylum wrapped comfortingly around my shoulders.

The real blanket that protects us, of course, is the embassy itself. The distance between security and death at this point is a trifling few feet, the negligible distance between fingers reaching out for a wall in despair and eyes that helplessly see those fingers torn from the wall, to be buried or broken, eyes that swear never to forget. Soon enough another sort of distance, another sort of helplessness, will put those eyes to the test: I know that these eyes of mine will travel far away, into the remote haven of foreign lands, the ultimate blanket and immunity that the embassy foretells.

I am already starting to learn the rules that govern the loss of a land. I am already starting to realize that my existence will be like that of all exiles who survive, like the multitude of Latin American exiles around me in the embassy, who came to Chile from their own frustrated revolutions, who have already lived the future that awaits me, all of us mercilessly defined by those who remain behind, our existence contrasted to that of those who did not or could not flee, our existence justified by the help we can bring to those who died in our stead yesterday or who risk death in our stead tomorrow. Exiles are haunted by the fingers grasping at a wall, grasping at a distance that has become immense and almost insurmountable.

That distance allowed me to bear witness to the outrage being perpetrated back home; indeed, demanded that I carry out that task. And yet, from the moment of departure, that witnessing would inevitably be indirect. Even before I depart, the embassy wall has insulated me from the person who was trying to escape. I cannot say who he was, what was his fate, how it was that he came to throw his bundle over the wall. Later, as the space grows, as miles and time zones separate me from the Chile where men reach a wall and then die before they can jump over it, I will have contact only through newspaper articles, letters, cassettes, a fleeting photo, a guarded voice on the phone, stories murmured by the newest refugees or released prisoners or, eventually, friends who come to visit, everything far, lived and told by someone else. This is one of the great paradoxes of exile: the sanctuary I have found, the very sanctuary that guarantees that a voice has survived, simultaneously cuts that voice off from direct access to the land it is responsible for keeping alive, the land that demands to be transmitted to others.

But you do what you can.

And now, more than twenty years later, I tell the story of the blanket that someone I never saw sent me as if from heaven. I tell his story even if I will never know what became of him. I tell his story because it is the only way I can thank him for keeping me warm, the only way I can mourn him and keep him alive, send him this blanket of words that cannot save him from whatever happened, what already happened to him and to me so long ago.

PAUL WEST

# A Missing Star

Some voices impose themselves on posterity. My old friend, astronomer Carl Sagan, had such a voice: a tutored baritone, no doubt practiced in bathroom or laboratory, bouncing about among tile and glass, a calmative among the wets and clinks, the squeaky faucets, and the hoarse Bunsen burners. In the old days, when he never wore a suit, when we chatted about salary, Swinburne, and stars, the voice wasn't quite so manicured, so crisply mahogany in hue; and much later I wondered how that voice had fared when, reduced to heart-broken banality, he found himself saying to his dying father, "Take care." I knew his parents quite well, having become a fan of his mother's potato pancakes, of his father's burly wit; besides, his mother, Rachel, knew my books and urged them upon her son, who complied.

I live in a house only a short downhill walk from where

Carl now lies horizontal in a box, still a neighbor I suppose, motionless and dumb. And this new image of him fills me with ontological horror. His cherished cosmos did this to him at sixty-two, renewing Beckett's warning that death does not require us to keep a day free in the calendar. We abide its whim and its deadly design with what the Greeks called *frike*, a hair-raising shudder, and then hope to think of something else.

There is such haste to get them out of sight, certainly in Carl's religion, Judaism, even in temperate climes. Perhaps this is a more majestic version of our eagerness to warehouse ourselves as soon as we begin to age and no longer fit the eugenic paradigm of flawless maturity in the best of possible worlds. Sometimes, when it's snowy in the Finger Lakes, bodies await burial for months, hoarded up until the ground softens again, and I wonder about the housing of the dead in attic, outhouse, or gazebo, erect as in a catacomb or at some wakes, remembering a Hemingway story in which the bereaved hang a hurricane lamp on the deceased's frozen lower jaw.

There is something to be said for keeping the dead with us longer, hygiene be damned, so that the state they have entered becomes a piece of the real, like their loquacity, their sarcasm, their charm. Death, about which, as distinct from dying, we know too little, deserves to be better known, looked at with less disgust, almost as if it were what Aristotle, who knew everything, called a form of imitation without a name. They are trying to be like us and something holds them back, but they are wonderful in their hidebound striving.

Could we bear it? Could it be worse than living among those compound ghosts of the departed, cobbled together, in Carl's case, from the sailcloth crackle of his brand-new yellow swim shorts as he once plunged into the waves off Cocoa

Beach, the way he held a tape recorder to his chin as if shaving, the empathetic irony in his voice when he called me long-distance on my fiftieth birthday, I in darkest Pittsburgh, to reassure and fortify, he four years younger? Perhaps what horrifies us is the smidgen of death we allow ourselves, shunting it away from us like the plague. We suffer from synecdoche, taking part for whole, when we need corporeal impact—no more memorial services sanitized by the body's having gone. Maybe death comes first, then the dying begins; or death happens in a sea of dying that both precedes and follows it.

There is another problem, particularly in this man's case. Seen often on TV, he may have achieved a replica of immortality anyway, in which case, according to what I have just written, we need to see his body even more—weekly—on the tube, lying in state like the Crab Nebula. I think I saw him as much in life as ever on TV, perhaps more, so I have a double image of him to cope with, complicated even further by the fact that, only months before he died, I finished an autobiographical novel in which he figured as the character Raoul Bunsen, who talked a pair of lovers into astronomy, taking them along with him to Cape Canaveral, as it then was, the Jet Propulsion Lab in Pasadena, and many other holy of holies usually denied to novelists and poets. In this love story haunted by astronomy, he lived again before he even died, all the way through what I think of as his golden days, when he excelled at the graces of the amateur, the fervent savant, before the prospect of nuclear winter filled his mind.

The upshot of all this is that, at least until the novel gets published, I will have his remainder, or rather my purloined version of his body, on my premises, more or less to myself, which is better than trying to deal with him as a cloud of disembodied memories. Congealed in cold print, not by him but by me, he will haunt me still, because I know now, as I did not while writing the novel, that the real person, of whom Raoul Bunsen is an imitation, a translation even, lies a little way downhill from the house, oddly dispossessed of himself, a star that winked out, whose image continues to travel through space.

ALBERT GOLDBARTH

# Parnassus

Technically I was a man.

This spindly squeaky thing with the adam's apple accent was, by virtue of being thirteen and bar mitzvahed, a technical man.

And so the phone call came: they needed a tenth for a minyan. Nathan Kaplan—I remembered Mr. Kaplan, didn't I?—needed to say the *yiskor* prayers for his wife, and if I weren't there in attendance, lending my lame but official singsong to these *daveners*, the God Who Demanded a Threshold of Ten would never turn His Ear of Ears to their puff of plaintive Kaplan imploration.

I didn't *want* to; but I went. I wanted to—what? Watch television? Play with my willie? Stare at a smear of clouds and wish a burning pinpoint of myself up through them, into the currents of outer space? The angsts and overbrimmings of being technically a man are many. In any case, yes, I went.

There isn't much more to say. They were ancient and stale of breath, and silked and fringed in the ritual synagoguewear, and I stood among them, following their lead and saying *amen* whenever someone's gnarled radish of a finger thumped the word out in my opened book. I loaned my voice, it took its place in a single wing of voice that made its technical way through the top of the ionosphere, and into a realm of shimmering off the scale of human perception. This is why I believe in the muses, of course.

There were nine of them.

And ever since, if I've been invited to join them for a moment, to sing along as a tenth—though they may have scraped the bottom of the barrel to get my number, I go.

KINERETH GENSLER

# In Between

In the 1930s, when I was growing up, my father had a winter job and a summer job. Winters, he was a professor of education at the Hebrew University in Jerusalem; summers, he and my mother ran a Jewish summer camp in Maine. Earlier, we lived in Chicago. We traveled enough so that I had whooping cough in Maine, measles on board ship, and scarlet fever in Jerusalem. Sea travel had its own slow rhythm, its own fascination, discomforts and boredom for a child who did part of her growing up on ships. There was the chance to meet people from the countries you would be traveling through, time to adapt to a new way of living, to whatever was coming.

Traveling on the margins of a continent soon to be engulfed by war, I saw Italian troops on their way to Ethiopia. I made friends with Dorit, a young German teenager who told me that her father was Jewish and her mother Aryan. She lived near Dachau and probably died in the concentration camp there. I danced with a German jewelry salesman who soon thereafter must have been drafted into the Wehrmacht. I was immersed every spring and fall in two different countries, different languages and alphabets, different smells: the Maine woods, Jaffa oranges. In between, the sharp Barcolene odor of ships' lavatories. And then there was the deep kinesthetic sense of being *en route*, that pivoting of one's whole self, backwatering as ocean liners do when they turn at the coasts.

WILLIAM KLOEFKORN

## A Sense of Water

*We father you not—we love you—there is perfection*
  *in you also,*
*You furnish your parts toward eternity,*
*Great or small, you furnish your parts toward the soul.*
—WALT WHITMAN, "CROSSING BROOKLYN FERRY"

Recently—to celebrate a special anniversary—my wife and I
indulged ourselves with a Caribbean cruise. Our enormous
liner exuded more glitz and dissipation than Father Lightbody
might fairly be expected to expiate in a month of Sundays. We
sunbathed and we shopped and we rubbernecked our fellow
adventurers until fathom by fathom our corporeal vessels over-
flowed. Strobe and twang, belly and bikini and gratuity and
the lift and the fall, the lilt and the sway of the ship, the creak
and the groan and the shivering of more than timbers. At

times I felt returned to the waters of the womb, at other times freshly relieved of it—out of its cradle, Walt Whitman, endlessly rocking.

The cruise was fun. The brochures bright almost as my grandmother's seed catalogs said the voyage would be, and it was: in the exercise room, hope in one hand and a rum swizzler in the other, I walked a treadmill—body moving, going nowhere; at regular intervals the Captain from the bridge asked for our attention in a Latino voice so stentorian, and over an intercom so devoted to volume, we had no choice but to cover our ears and listen. Latitude and longitude and rectitude. Twenty knots in the general direction of Eden. And beneath the keel, more than one thousand feet directly down, the floor of the Caribbean.

*If there is magic on this planet, it is contained in water.* Each evening as the sun neared the horizon my wife and I studied the blueness of the Caribbean, took notes on it in silence without pad or pencil, filing the notes away somewhere in the handiest cortex of the brain. If her sense of water runs as deep as mine, I pity the poor bastard boatswain whose paycheck will be deferred until he sounds it.

One of those evenings, recording notes without taking them, I remembered a news account I had run across a year or so ago. It appeared under the general heading of Human Interest, and it told of a Baptist preacher somewhere in the Deep South who in the process of baptizing his sparse congregation at the edge of a river held one of them under a bit too long; when the frightened sinner floundered, the preacher released him and he drifted away screaming and soon located the principal current and drowned. A compelling combination of the mortal and the immortal, I thought, flesh shouting its reluctance into the cool quotient of the spirit. And I wondered if the baptism had been sufficiently and well enough performed for it to have taken hold and thus last, like a child-hood vaccination. Trinity: code name for the testing of the atomic bomb in New Mexico. In the name of the Father, and of the Son, and . . .

And I wondered too about my own Father—dead since 9 December 1990, his brown Dodge broadsided by a drunk—who with two fingers missing on his right hand had grappled me out of Simpson's Pond in south-central Kansas to arrange me on a pallet of bunchgrass to pump water from me as if from a cistern: to what extent might he have sacrificed a part of himself for me?

God knows I don't know. I know only that at sunset the Caribbean, though somewhat vaster and deeper and bluer than Simpson's Pond, should not permit itself to become uppity; it can only become larger than the sum of its parts when those parts come together. Above it meanwhile the Rockies in Colorado and in Wyoming's Snowy Range are con-tributing their parts drop by eternal drop to the ultimate cis-tern, to the myriad touchstones of wetness, these to be joined by the Sandhill waters of the North and Middle Loups in Nebraska, all then (but not all finally) snaking and braiding their way to become John Niehardt's Missouri, John yielding himself willingly to become Mark Twain's Mississippi, Mississippi then losing itself to the Caribbean, and that to the greater Atlantic, loss in its own inscrutable way thus returning a profit, a dividend, while my kinfolk, those creatures of the deep both bone and otherwise that I cannot see but know are there, swim on, swim on.

PATTIANN ROGERS

# Fury and Grace

Shoal Creek, near Joplin, Missouri, where I grew up, is, for me, the archetype of all creeks. We went to see Shoal Creek often when I was young, like visiting a highly interesting acquaintance who lived a strange but purposeful life. The creek was always there, more or less in its same place, doing its mud-and-fish, worn-rock-and-ruffled-rapids, racing act.

I could wade through the clear waters where it widened near a small dam, bend down, and look from my world through a silver, reflective boundary into a world that was forced to remain within that boundary—tiny black snails like spots on the stones, fat tadpoles that seemed just heads with wispy tails, crawdads propelling backwards to hide beneath muddy leaves and muck, olive-green minnows so narrow and rock-colored that they were almost invisible until they flicked and moved as one body from sun to shadow.

And when I looked up again into the world of air and sky, it seemed I had been existing in another life, among alien creatures whom I nevertheless knew and regarded with respect.

I occasionally swam in Shoal Creek, learning of it in another way, standing waist-deep in its murky water, pushing against its force on my body, or sitting in its shallow rapids making it rear up, ruffle and surge against my back. Who was it? It came and went constantly yet was always present.

McClellan Park was situated on a steep hill, a high cliff above Shoal Creek, a cliff covered with rocky bluffs and caves typical of the area. A picnic at McClellan Park always involved a precarious hike down the hill, everyone slipping on rocks and gravel, skidding and grabbing bushes and trees to keep from falling. I held onto my dad. At the bottom we would walk for a while beside the creek, which ran close to the hill, pressing against the rise of the land. My dad skipped rocks over the surface of the water, big leaps and then smaller. My brother and I tried.

A favorite story of my dad's was the time my brother, six years old, started running down the hill and couldn't stop, shouting and yelling. My dad, running after him, barely grabbed him by one arm, swinging him out over the creek just before he plunged into its deep, rushing waters.

Once we went in the rain to see Shoal Creek mad and powerful, high over its banks, its white froth climbing and fighting against the thick poplars marking its old boundaries. It rolled and thrashed over its single-lane bridge. We were consigned to viewing the flooding from one side, many cars lined up before the impassable crossing. People in raincoats and boots stood around outside their cars watching in amazement, proclaiming in low voices, with reverence and respect, as if Shoal Creek were justified in this show of frightening rebellion.

But I love Shoal Creek most, I think, because I first learned about the bodies of boys while parked beside it at the end of dirt fishing lanes, the sound of its life continually cresting and flowing, swelling and rhythmic in the background among the whispers and laughters and joys of those nights. The affirmation and promise of moving water has been present with me since, in everything I've ever experienced of sexual love.

The being and cadence of Shoal Creek is part of who I am, defining both fury and grace, influencing the pace of my passions, shaping the undercurrent of my sleep, resonant always in the waking motion and music of my language and my thought.

JOHN MCPHEE

# Swimming with Canoes

I grew up in a summer camp—Keewaydin—whose special-
ty was canoes and canoe travel. At the home base, near
Middlebury, Vermont, were racks and racks of canoes, at least
a hundred canoes—E.M. Whites and Chestnuts, mainly.
They were very good wood-and-canvas keeled or keelless
canoes, lake or river canoes. We were in them every day wherever we were, in and out of Vermont. We were like some sort
of crustaceans with our rib-and-planking exoskeletons, and to
this day I do not feel complete or safe unless I am surrounded
by the protective shape of a canoe.

Now and again, Keewaydin let us take our canoes not so
much onto the water as into it, during swim period. We went
swimming with our canoes. We jounced. Jouncing is the art of
propelling a canoe without a paddle. You stand up on the
gunwales near the stern deck and repeatedly flex and unflex

your knees. The canoe rocks, slaps the lake, moves forward. Sooner or later, you lose your balance and fall into the water, because the gunwales are slender rails and the stern deck is somewhat smaller than a pennant. From waters deeper than you were tall, you climbed back into your canoe. If you think that's easy, try it.

After three or four splats, and with a belly pink from hauling it over gunwales, you lost interest in jouncing. What next? You sat in your canoe and deliberately overturned it. You leaned hard to one side, grabbed the opposite gunwale, and pulled. Out you went, and into the water. This was, after all, swim period. Now you rolled your canoe—an action it resists far less when it is loaded with water. You could make your canoe spiral like a football inside the lake.

And before long you found the air pocket. Having jounced and spiralled to the far end of your invention span, you ducked beneath the surface and swam in under your upside-down canoe. You rose slowly to miss a thwart—feeling above you, avoiding a bump on the head—and then your eyes, nose and mouth were in air, among chain-link streaks of white and amber light, the shimmers of reflection in a quonset grotto. Its vertical inches were few but enough. Your pals got in there with you and your voices were tympanic in the grotto. Or you just hung out there by yourself. With a hand on a thwart, and your feet slowly kicking, you could breathe normally, see normally, talk abnormally, and wait indefinitely for a change of mood. You were invisible to the upside, outside world. Even more than when kneeling in a fast current, you were one with your canoe.

Kneeling in a fast current. Once in a while, we went to what is now called Battell Gorge, north of Middlebury, to learn how to deal with really fast, pounding, concentrated flow. Otter Creek, there, undergoes an abrupt change in physiographic character. After meandering benignly through the marshes, woodlots, and meadows of the Champlain Valley, it encounters a large limestone outcrop, which it deeply bisects. By a factor of three or four, the stream narrows and the water squeezes into humps, haystacks, souse holes, and standing waves as it drops ten feet in a hundred yards. Then it emerges from the high limestone walls and the darkness of overhanging hemlocks into the light of a pool so wide it seems to be a pond.

Like horse people, we showed up some distance above the head of the gorge with trailers—racked trailers that each carried seven canoes. The gorge was a good place to learn how to deal with canoes in white water because it was violent but short. In that narrow, roaring flume, you didn't have to choose the best route—didn't have to look for what the *voyageurs* called the *fil d'eau*. There was pretty much one way to go. But you got the sense of a canoe flying in three dimensions; and the more you did it the slower it seemed, the shoot separating itself into distinct parts, as if you were in a balloon rising in sunlight and falling in the shadows of clouds.

One time, when I was about twelve, I went into the gorge in a very old canoe that was missing its stern seat. (We didn't take the better boats there.) Two of us were paddling it. I was kneeling against the stern thwart, which was so far back it was only eight or ten inches from gunwale to gunwale, the size of my young butt. My right knee was on the canoe's ribs, and my right leg extended so far back that my foot was wedged in the V of the stern when the bucking canoe turned over. Billy Furey was my partner, and we were doing all we could to keep things even, but whatever we did wasn't good enough, and we flipped near the top of the gorge. Billy was ejected. Among the countless wonders of the simple design of the native American canoe is the fact that it ejects its paddlers when it capsizes.

This one could not eject me, because my foot was stuck. I struggled to pull the foot free, but it wouldn't come. Upside down in billows of water, I could not get out. Understand: I have a life-long tendency to panic. Almost anything will panic me—health, money, working with words. Almost anything—I'm here to tell you—but an overturned canoe in a raging gorge. When I was trapped in there, if panic crossed by mind it went out the other side. I had, after all, time and time again been swimming with canoes. There was a purpose in letting us do that—a thought that had never occurred to me. After I realized I was caught and was not going to be coming out from under that canoe, I reached for the stern quarter-thwart, took hold of it, and pulled my body upward until my eyes, nose, and mouth were in the grotto. There, in the dancing light, I rode on through the gorge, and when the water calmed down at the far end I gave the canoe half a spiral and returned to the open sunlight.

BERNARD COOPER

# Train of Thought

I searched through *Brewer's Dictionary of Phrase and Fable* to find information on the expression *train of thought*, but found nothing under either *train* or *thought*. Certainly the origin of that expression couldn't have predated the invention of the locomotive in 1801. Before 1801, when a person was alert to a clattering onslaught of thoughts, big overloaded boxcars of thought, thoughts linked together and barreling by, what expression would that person have used? Take Voltaire, for instance, who was reputed to write while consuming more than thirty cups of coffee a day. (No wonder Candide endures misfortunes from pratfall to flogging in a mere ninety pages.) Perhaps Voltaire, pen ashudder, likened his thoughts to stampeding horses or a swarm of bees. Had there been trains in the 1700s, it's not impossible that Voltaire himself would have been the one to coin the phrase *train of thought*, though *coin* is far too sluggish a verb to describe how that metaphor would have heaved itself upon him, careened through his imagination, preceded and followed by a dozen thoughts of equal interest, as he paced the dining car, coffee cup in hand, Parisian townships surging past the window, blurred as drops of gouache in water.

The etymology of this expression stems from the industrial age, that reign of clanking mechanical contraptions, pistons pumping, conveyor belts conveying. But it's a sadly lacking expression for the post-industrial age, when voluminous amounts of information are flicked across continents in nanoseconds and practically every week physicists proclaim the existence of a subatomic particle that is smaller and shorter-lived and more elusive than the particle thought to be the fundamental building block of matter the day before. And what with frequent technological advances in the rapid transmission of words and images, from telex to modem to satellite dish, even the *lightning* in the term *lightning fast* seems feeble and inadequate, a waning glow in our vocabulary.

So the question is how to update the phrase *train of thought*, how to dust it off, streamline its antiquated angles, how to make it purr like a monorail, swoop through the beleaguered imagination with the thrust of the Concorde surpassing sound. You can replace the cowcatcher with a nose cone, use plutonium instead of coal, fit the caboose with a booster rocket, but that won't make it modern for long. At the rate science proceeds, rockets and missiles may one day seem like buffalo—slow, endangered grazers in the black pasture of outer space.

It was only thirty years ago that my father read me asleep from *The Big Book of Trains*. Each illustrated page explained the function of a single car—hopper, tank, flatcar, stock car—and I'd pull away from the station of my waking toward the deep, improbable twilight of dreams. In the realm of dreams there was a train of thought too, but wheeling freely off its track, strange fumes spewing from the smokestack. In one seminal dream from my childhood I was on a train with a woman who was dressed in an enormous satin skirt. I was sitting on her lap and we ladled cupfuls of cool water into each other's mouths. Her petticoats crackled whenever I lifted the cup to her lips. "Where are we going?" I asked her. "To the city," she said, "where the rustling of a woman's skirt sounds the same as the rain." I remember that dream because it was the first from which I awoke with a phrase intact, a phrase that withstood the morning light, and I fell in love with words.

Watching TV when I was ten, I saw a lengthy succession of freight rolling past a boy my age. After it passed, he recited for a reporter the serial number and product name printed on the side of each car: Alpine Timber, 56782; Dromedary Products, 92301; Bandy Brothers Cattle, 94933. I envied the reach and precision of his memory, even after I learned that the boy was an "idiot savant," incapable of tying his shoelaces or naming the country in which he lived. I wonder, would it be so bad to be stunted in the face of ordinary tasks if one, just one train in your entire life, rumbled by and scored your mind with its indelible impression, its manifold numbers and assonant names, its raucous livestock, ripe oranges, mounds of ore, its pattern of sunlight bursting through the slats?

So many streets in downtown Los Angeles are embedded with unused railroad track. On rainy days, they gleam like the trail a snail leaves, veering off, aimless tangents, miles of metal sunk in puddles. Perhaps if you viewed them from the fortieth floor of the new Conoco Corporation headquarters, they would form the letters of a brief lament, a poem composed of cursive rails, about history washed away by rain, about the city's relentless change, the wrecking balls, boarded windows, haunted train yards, extinct machines.

S T E V E   H E L L E R

# Swan's Way, 1998

The morning after I return from a conference in Portland, I discover, nestled in the budding grass on our front lawn beside the Sunday paper, a white plastic swan. The bird wears a demure expression, as if it were floating peacefully on a lily pond near the River Seine. Instead, the bird in my yard is surrounded by a tiny white plastic picket fence. On its breast, it bears a sign: THIS IS A HOUSEWARMING POULTRY. IT MAKES ITS WAY FROM NEWLY REMODELED HOME TO NEWLY REMODELED HOME, LAYING EGGS WITH MESSAGES INSIDE. CONGRATULATIONS ON FINALLY GETTING BACK INTO THE (NEW) PLACE. CHRISTMAS, RIGHT?

I smile. This is the end of March. We'd been in a rental since early September and had moved back two days before my trip. On the opposite side of the yard stand two previous tokens from anonymous welcomers: a pair of plastic pink flamingos and a ceramic toad playing the cello.

Snuggled in the swan's hollow back lie a clutch of multi-colored plastic eggs. I lift out a blue one and crack it open to read: "When a person (re)moves into his home, how is that such a grand occasion? This was not post-flood, post-earth-quake, or post-fire." How grand indeed? I open a yellow one: "When you hear the laughing next door, it's not the birds they're chuckling at."

Self-conscious now, I cock my head and listen. But the morning is cool and still, the tall oak trees in the park across the street barely breathing. Better to open the remaining eggs inside the house with the rest of the family, in the privacy of deep green walls and oak bookshelves in the new library, where laughter echoes only from the pages of familiar tales. Mary and the boys are sleeping, exhausted from four days of unpacking I shamefully skipped out on. My time has come, they've all informed me, beginning this very morning, the moment Rachael stirs in her crib. It's only fair and right, of course, and I am more than ready, armed now with the col-lected sardonic wisdom of a plastic bird.

But as I bend down to scoop out the remaining eggs, at least a dozen or so, something happens. For a moment my eyes fix on the graceful curve of the swan's neck, and an odd noise disturbs the parkside peace: a sizzling, buzzing sound, like an electrical short of some kind. I look around to discover its source—then realize this sound exists only in my head. The only sound my ears actually hear is the languorous drone of a truck grinding its way along the far edge of the park. The only scent I smell is the fresh dew on the green lawn. My mouth waters, but there is no flavor of madeleine cake and tea, noth-ing on my tastebuds to inspire what is now happening inside my head. But as I stare at the plastic swan's neck and listen to the buzzing sound in my brain, I recognize at once where my mind's eye has already taken me: across four decades to another swan. This one a blue arc of humming neon, blazing against a dark sky. Immediately beneath the electric bird, etched in buzzing blue, two words: SWAN MOTEL.

These swans no longer exist: neither the shimmering blue bird nor the motel itself, though in the early 1960s both burned brightly in my family's future. In 1953, when I was four, my father was injured while working as an electrician for the Frisco Railroad in Oklahoma City. A conductor signaled an engineer the all-clear to start up a freight train just as my father was stepping off the caboose where he'd been finishing up some rewiring. The tug of the diesel engine made the caboose lurch, and Father lost his balance and tumbled off the steps. As he fell, a loop in his overalls caught on an assist handle, and the combined forces flung him beneath the train. The loop continued to hold as the train slowly picked up speed, dragging him over the track ties just in front of the train's last set of steel wheels, shattering bone after bone in a matter of seconds—until at last a gandydancer named Big Foot Pete Yuri saw what was happening and pulled him free.

Father spent much of the following three years in and out of hospitals and clinics, healing bones and back. At one point it appeared he might be crippled for life, but in time he recovered well enough to get around, even to resume his career as an electrician. But not with the railroad, which he sued. In 1958 the Frisco settled with him for $20,000, a decent bit of money in those days. The lawyer who represented Father in the suit talked him into investing the money in a motel in Fort Smith, Arkansas. *You put up the dollars; my wife and I will run the motel*, the attorney said. *You'll be the silent partner. We can't miss.* Mother was skeptical from the beginning. *What kind of lawyer wants to run a motel?* she asked Father again and again. *Look, he got the money for us,* was Father's repeated answer. *He stuck with me for three years to do it.* And so, in an

act of gratitude and faith, Father made the worst decision of
his life.

Now, as I stare at the plastic swan nestled in my yard and
the blue neon swan gleaming in my mind's eye, something
else happens. I don't know why, I'm sure I'll never know exactly why, but all at once both swans disappear and I find myself
stretched out on the back seat of Father's old gray beetle-black
1950 Dodge, which he was still driving in 1961, the green
plaid bench seat ragged and musty, but comfortable enough
for a boy tired from a long drive. I'm old enough to remember
things now, and I know where we are: heading east toward
Fort Smith along Route 64, passing through towns with
names like Gore, Vian, and Sallisaw. I don't know our precise
location because it's night and the lights of the previous town
have already blurred away. Mother and Father think I'm sleeping. I can tell from their conversation, which is about the
motel and me.

*The Coefields are stealing us blind*, Mother says. The
tremor in her voice tells me she wants to cry, but mother never
cries. *This is the last trip to Fort Smith. We're going to lose everything. Everything, even the house.*

*You're right*, Father admits. *You were right all along. At least
the boy had his Christmas.*

*He needs more than Christmas.* Mother is silent for a while.
I listen to the hum of the tires over blacktop, feel the drum-
ming echo of the road through the bench seat. *Maybe he needs
a brother or a sister*, Mother says suddenly. *Maybe we should
adopt.*

I dig my fingernails into the ragged cloth of the seat. I
don't want a brother or a sister. It's too late for that. But I close
my eyes and say nothing.

Out of the darkness, Father speaks for me. *The boy likes
being alone. He's used to it.*

Mother sighs, a melancholy sound I recognize as defeat. *Maybe you're right. I just . . . I just want him to have a full life, that's all.*

I have a full life! I want to cry out. But it's too late: when I open my eyes, my parents and the beetle-black Dodge have vanished. So has the electric blue swan. The swan that stares back at me now has plastic eyes and a clutch of plastic eggs that tell my fortune. I gather each one carefully into my arms and go into the house to cook my family breakfast.

TENAYA DARLINGTON

# Dream Houses

The house I grew up in had one bathroom, a tub in it. No shower. The rooms were small, more like clubhouses than rooms, and the basement, which was divided into my father's music room on one side and our playroom on the other, had been decorated by the previous owners who were local football fans. Hence the red and yellow shag. It was a make-do house. A small ranch-style with a high-sloping driveway on a corner lot. Every year there was talk of putting in a shower, taking down the foil wallpaper over the stove, getting rid of that awful paneling downstairs, and fixing the part of the ceiling that buckled. But every year, the same reply from my parents: *we're waiting for our dream house, we'll probably move next year.*

Three years ago, my parents finally moved. After twenty, yes, twenty temporary years, the perfect house in the woods came onto the market: a modern-looking flat-roof with wood siding stained a cool gray. Inside, the back wall is all glass and there are skylights. A huge stone fireplace pipes warmth into the heating ducts to warm the whole house. When my brother and I visit during the holidays we sleep in large rooms that overlook a wooded ravine, snow falling against timber, and somewhere in the distance, a barred owl croons for a matching call. It's the sort of house people smoke pipes in and writers write in. The low-slung pine beams on the upper floor make it feel less like a house real people live in and more like a ski lodge, a retreat for dreamers. And so we watch our parents float in front of the window, my mother in her wool clogs, my father in his moccasins, hands wrapped around chunky mugs of coffee. It feels like a commercial. When my brother and I swap hellos going in and out of the bathroom (with its massager shower and all-white matchingness), I can't help but think of Best Western.

In the afternoons at the dream house, we do dream things: walk down the ravine to where there is a river with a small island, find a swatch of fox fur on the path, climb a fallen tree that looks like a reclining woman (two big branches like her legs, two big knots like her breasts). My brother is in college now and I am several years out, yet we act like kids in those woods, running through the trees, skipping rocks, delighting in a nest or a set of deer prints, and dragging home a huge sheet of bark to plant in front of the house like a flag. We live on hot chocolate and hard cookies sent to us by an aunt in Switzerland, and in the evening, at my mother's insistence, we roast hot dogs and marshmallows in front of the fire and eat lying down.

My mother gets a little teary during these visits. *It's a shame,* she'll say, shaking her head, *that we didn't live here when you were children. Think how differently you'd look back on your childhood.* What she doesn't know is this: sometimes at night, my brother and I will go for a drive. We'll drive across town, sleet pressing itself against the windshield and the radio tuned to some eighties station, and we'll park in front of our old house. It's in a neighborhood of other small houses like it where, at one time, we knew all the families. Mrs. Berry in the pale blue house who used to give us divinity; the Clarks in the white colonial with the playhouse and fish pond; the Phillips in the vanilla two-story who threw birthday parties for their bulldogs; the Zimmermans across from them who took us arrowhead-hunting on rainy Saturdays; Mr. Cook, diagonally, who helped my father on the car and had a cat lovingly named "Cat."

Our old house looks at us like a dejected pet in a pound. It knows we are sitting outside in the car, sharing a bag of Raisinets from the glove compartment. Lights are on in two windows, like eyes—figures passing in the hallway like our own shadows still lingering, still fighting over who gets to take the first bath. Our breath freezes like blank captions in a cartoon of ourselves, and I think of the one bathroom with the ledge where I used to sit and paint my toes. My mother would be taking a bubble bath, my father reading *Stereo Review* on his throne, my brother brushing his teeth and making faces at himself in the mirror while the dog slept on a pile of towels. The whole family crowded in one bathroom, its door never closed. It was the center of everything, the stage with the tubside seating where we watched my mother cut her hair, my father trim his beard. Aside from going to the mall two blocks east, it was the social hub. I can't imagine us like that now, hanging out, sharing gossip in one of the dream bathrooms with its three-way mirrors, fader switches, and cold floors.

My brother and I drive back across town, a trail of tire tracks in the snow connecting the old house with the new. *Remember the dent in the door from your moon boot? Remember the mark on the ceiling above the oven that we always thought was a trap door? Remember the space under the stairs where we hoarded Flintstones vitamins and ate them like candy?* When we return, the house is dark, our parents asleep at their end of the house. We pat the walls, hunting for a light switch.

The truth about dream houses, especially dream houses out in the woods that are purchased late in life, is that they are like empty beehives, grandiose combs with elaborate compartments but without the dreams to fill them. When I go home to visit, I enjoy the beautiful view, the way the seasons pervade the living room—the changing leaves like changing wallpaper—and I love that raccoons come to the window in the den at night and look in, but they are no substitute for having neighbors. And when my brother and I leave after the holidays are over, I envision my parents rattling around in a house as empty as it is beautiful. I see them spread out in distant corners, my father downstairs in his office, my mother upstairs at her desk, both of them looking out through binoculars at a pheasant or a grouse and seeing only snowflakes magnified many times to look like moths. And beyond that: nothing, and more nothing, and beyond that, perhaps a dream, or the footprints of a dream leading to another house.

EDWIDGE DANTICAT

# Waking Dreams

The filmmaker Jonathan Demme directed a short radio drama that I wrote to be broadcast on a station in Port-au-Prince. It was the story of a father who kills himself because he feels he is not living up to his own dreams or his family's expectations of him. Jonathan wanted my father to be in the radio drama. We knew that Papi would never agree to play the father role, which would require that he speak half the dialogue in the story. So we asked him to play a very small part as a factory foreman.

When the time came to record, I was terrified about having my father listen to the voices of the mother and the child in the story. They literally *loved* the father to death. Without realizing it, they drove him to extremes to please them and finally made him feel unworthy of their admiration. I most feared for my father hearing this line spoken by the actor playing the child: "I would rather die than be like my father whose life meant nothing."

Every time the actor spoke the line I saw my father wince. I knew his mannerisms well enough to read his expression. *Is that what she thinks of me?* I scolded myself, repeating the refrain of one of my closest friends. "Why can't you write happy things?"

On that day I wished I had written something happy, something closer to my father, truer to his own life. It's been said that most writers betray someone at some point in their lives. I felt that I had betrayed my father by not writing about a father who was more of a kindred spirit to him. Since I had the choice, I should have created a fighter, a survivor, a man who would never take the easy way out of life because he wanted to see "his children end up well."

In the studio that day, my father sat in a corner and practiced his few lines as the factory foreman. He even joked with Jonathan about finally getting his chance to be the boss. When his turn came, he recited the lines. He went over them a few times before they had the right timbre.

Later, I wanted to explain. In the car on the way home, I said, "Papi, you know it was a story."

He nodded. "Of course, of course. I understand."

I worried that I had wounded him, that somehow he'd feel that everything he's done in his life has been for nothing. But a few weeks later, I saw him put the tape of the radio play in his car, before heading out to work in his taxi at 4:00 A.M. He listened and he laughed while waiting for his engine to warm up.

I remembered Jonathan saying, "You should have seen your old man's face in the studio. He was beaming with pride." I could not see it in the studio, but that day as my father sat in his cab listening, I could see that he was seeing the obvious difference between that father and himself.

When I was a little girl, mad at my father for leaving me, I used to have a recurring dream. I was running in a very dense crowd looking for someone whose face I didn't know but whom I expected to recognize on sight. The people in the crowd had no faces except the one man at the very end, who was my father. Never have I seen my father's face so clearly as when I saw it in that dream. Even in person, he's never been so alive yet so serene, so beautiful.

Now, when I look at him over my mother's head through their bedroom window on Saturday mornings at 4:00 A.M., I always have to remind myself not to compare my real father to that dream. The man in that dream was not there. This father is. And as my father is sitting in his car waiting for his engine to warm up, I always wonder what is he thinking about? Is he thinking about the past, about that little girl who loved him so much that she was afraid to go near him for fear he might leave her again? Perhaps my father has now surrendered all that to the present, to the car, the engine, the cold, to the itch of balding, aging, and the resulting eczema.

I once asked Papi if he ever had any dreams about my brother André and me when we were still young in Haiti.

"Of course, of course," he said, "but there are too many to tell."

He did not just have the kind of dreams that you have while sleeping, he said. He had waking dreams; he saw our faces everywhere.

"And now every once in a while I see you in my waking dreams," I told him. "One day I would like to write about that."

"Yeah? If that is true, then will you do something for me?" he asked. "When you write about me give me some hair and decent skin. That will make me happy."

DIONISIO D. MARTÍNEZ

# A Sense of Wonder

It was an afternoon shortly after my family moved to Tampa nearly a decade after our exile from Cuba.

I was no different from other teens, wishing invisibility were an option when going anywhere with my parents, but that afternoon I willingly joined them for a matinee. A local movie theater was showing *Gone with the Wind* with subtitles in Spanish, and that made all the difference.

My parents hadn't seen the film in decades. My mother bought the Spanish translation of the book in the 1950s in Spain. She still speaks of that hardcover edition, which included photographs from the film. She laments its loss and asks me to look for it whenever I travel.

"Have you found the one with photographs?" she asks when I phone her at the end of one of my trips. This was, after all, her introduction to the American South that would become her home. It is one of those rare places where exile seems less real, or at least more bearable.

Long before I was born, my mom's affinity for Southern hospitality and the region's unique sense of decorum led to a vicarious rubbing of elbows with the characters of Tara. One of the advantages of an imagined life is that one can easily create a utopia. In her version of Tara, my mother is as close to the slaves as she is to Escarlata. (When I hear her call their names in Spanish, the story seems so intimate and the characters so real.)

That afternoon at the movies, my father and I watched my mother follow every frame, as if she could smell and feel the fire, as if she carried the full weight of the slaves' oppression, as if she were the air itself, the molecules of history flowing in and out of every character.

Years later, only months after my father's death, a disturbing incident pulled my mother back into reality. She awoke one morning and complained about something in one eye. I rushed her to the doctor. Once there, she insisted that I go to work. When I went to pick her up, she nonchalantly said she'd never see out of that eye again.

As shattering as my father's death had been for me, this was in some ways harder to accept. I prepared for my father's death the way, each summer, I prepare for hurricanes.

But the sudden news of my mother's partial blindness I can compare only to the 1971 Southern California earthquake, when we lived in Glendale and I was shaken out of my sleep.

Like a survivor in a Tennessee Williams tragedy, my mother, now seventy-one and living in Miami, has adapted to the loss of depth perception and to the serious limitations of her peripheral vision. A sixth sense—the sense of wonder—has blossomed in her like hibiscus after a long rain. Makes you wonder what she sees inside herself, how the inner world expands, how its distances are measured.

One day, visiting the Salvador Dalí Museum in St. Petersburg, Florida, I watched her much as I'd watched her years earlier at the movies with my father, and it seemed that she could travel far into any given canvas and come out with a perspective that would have enlightened Dalí himself.

She lives now in a place built partly by the architects of memory, partly by the architects of hope. Somehow, between the two, she manages to stay grounded and informed. She listens to the radio, even in her sleep, recording much of it. She has countless tapes of songs and call-in shows and editorials and interviews. She has static-filled broadcasts from Cuba.

Her eclectic taste has room for George Jones, Glenn Miller, Carlos Gardel, and even Creedence Clearwater Revival, whose music she discovered when we still lived in California and I started buying their records.

"Whatever happened to Creedence?" she'll ask me now and again. All the singers and musicians she admires perform on the same stage, where a hierarchy is out of the question, as it is in the utopian South of her mind.

In the real South, where she's afraid of thunder and is constantly reminded of what might have been if things in Cuba had taken a different turn in 1959, my mother rotates the radio very slowly, trying to get the best reception. She does it the way most people focus on a certain spot, trying to see it clearly. Her ears have become her eyes and she's making the most of it.

Suddenly, at this late stage in her life, she has started to write, and just as suddenly the words have disappeared. She has misplaced the pile of notebooks filled with lines and phrases she hopes to transform into poems.

A few weeks ago she called me at our family home in

Tampa to ask if I'd seen the notebooks. She called again last night. "Are you sure you've looked everywhere?"

My mother's universe is answering to a new set of laws: the search for her unfinished poems has taken the place and urgency of the search for that copy of *Gone with the Wind* with pictures from the film, which she lost in another country, where her eyesight was unaffected and the radio was just the incidental sound track of an otherwise silent life.

VERLYN KLINKENBORG

# All Over Again

There is evidence, scientists now say, that the capacity for speech arose in ancestral humans 400,000 years ago. The evidence is structural. The hole in the back of the skull, the hypoglossal canal, through which nerve fibers connect to the tongue is larger in early and modern humans than it is in chimpanzees and australopithecines, implying a more dexterous, more articulate tongue. We humans naturally think speaking divides us from the rest of the animals. So it is good to be reminded that the root of our difference and the source of so much proud philosophizing over the past 400 millennia lies in the material structure of the body itself.

For the last few years, I have been keenly aware of the physical nature of speech. My own voice had dwindled to a croak, rising sometimes to a wheeze, because of a painless, benign obstruction on one of my vocal cords. It had the same effect as a finger wrapped around a cello string—no vibration, no amplitude, no resonance. After a couple of failed operations, I went to a new surgeon who was able, bless her heart, to remove the obstruction completely. A week of silence passed, and then I made a few tentative noises. I sounded, to myself at least, like the Great and Mighty Oz. A rumbling rose from my chest. I could feel the vibration down through my feet, as though a train were passing.

Now, once a week, I sit in an office across 57th Street from Carnegie Hall and practice using my voice while a vocal therapist listens. I am making my tongue more dexterous. I read verses of Rossetti and Shakespeare aloud, enunciating the "n's," masticating the "m's," toothing the "t's." I say "red leather, yellow leather, blue leather" and "unique New York" again and again. I make siren noises and noises that even a chimp, with its inferior hypoglossal canal, could make. On my last visit, I sang "Row, Row, Row Your Boat," inserting a breath, per instruction, between "stream" and "merrily."

That night, across the street at Carnegie Hall, the great Swedish mezzo-soprano Anne Sofie von Otter appeared on stage, dressed in gold. After the applause fell away, her accompanist played a few supplicatory notes, and Ms. von Otter began quietly to sing one of Schubert's *lieder*. She sang more Schubert, then Sibelius, Mahler, Bizet, and then, at the end of the evening when the audience would not let her go, she sang "Memories of You" by Eubie Blake and "Slap That Bass" by George and Ira Gershwin.

It was, I think, the first time I ever heard the human voice for itself, listened past the music and heard the material structure on which it rested—the shaping of lips, teeth, tongue, the undergirding of breath, the very physicality of the body itself, which Ms. von Otter swayed and straightened as the phrasing demanded. She was as musical when she spoke to the audi-

ence as she was when she sang to it, and when she sang
Gershwin—"Zoom, zoom, zoom. Misery you got to go"—I
saw that behind the pleasure of the music there also lay the
pleasure, strange as it sounds, of making noise with the mouth
and lungs. As for us out there in the red plush seats, when Ms.
von Otter finished, we dumbly slapped one hand against the
other until our hands were sore.

# Messages

I am giving them different names. Late on a Sunday morning in summer, I was on my sundeck, feeling the sun, looking at grass, birds, blue sky, trees. Behind me, the door to the house was open. I heard the telephone ring. I was tense, listening. Everything was beautiful out here in the sun; I did not want to go inside and talk on the telephone. After four rings, the machine answered. I had Sinatra on the tape: he sang a line, then I spoke, then Sinatra sang another line. The caller listened to this for ten or twelve seconds, then talked. I did not know him; he sounded like a workingman, and in his voice were nuances of longing and affection. He said: "Betsy? This is Dave." I turned my wheelchair around and went through the door. "I haven't seen you in a while." I pushed down the hall. "If you'd like to get together, maybe we could meet tonight at that place we like." I turned into the dining room, wheeled toward the kitchen, to the telephone on the wall. "Okay, I hope I see you there." As I passed the telephone, I grabbed it, listened to a dial tone, wished he had left a number.

So she knew his number, or he did not want to be called. It could be adultery or other cheating. But she was not the unfaithful one; he would have hung up when Betsy did not answer. Maybe he was married, or living with a woman, and Betsy shared a place with a man who was neither her husband nor lover, so Dave heard my voice and still spoke to the machine. Maybe erotic love was not an element. But something had been in his voice, and he had not named the place where he wanted to be with her.

Next day at noon, I was on the deck, putting seed in the bird feeder. The phone rang and I did not move. Then I heard Dave's voice, and I turned and went through the door, calling "Don't hang up!" He said: "Betsy? This is Dave. I hear you were at that place we like last night, looking for me." I was in the dining room when he said: "I'll go there tonight, maybe you'll be there." I rolled quickly into the kitchen, reaching for the telephone; he hung up. Still I picked up the telephone. He was gone.

But where? Was he at work now? Would he go home after work, to shower and put on clean clothes, eat alone or with his wife, perhaps some children, or with a girlfriend? Then he would go to a bar I had never seen: it was large and dark. He would go there, with hope that was in his voice. Would Betsy be there? I imagined her tonight, in her thirties, wearing jeans and a shirt, wondering why he had not called, looking at her face in the bathroom mirror, applying lipstick and blush, then leaving her silent phone, and the rooms where she lived, and driving to the place they liked.

# e-mail

i had a wonderful valentine's day. my boy and i have this precarious relationship. in april he'll have finished with his BA and in august i'm leaving to go grow up. joshua isn't coming with me. but kisses and candles seem to make that matter less, they make admiration and loneliness look, feel so much like love.

he's my gabriel in tintoretto's painting of the annunciation. not that i'm some sort of holy mary but that he is announcing the rest of my life, declaring its potential, giving an explanation for my nervous acid stomach. he has given me a drive, a push, plain courage i needed to get going. he has also introduced me to more music, poems, stories and novels than anyone else i've ever met.

and of course he's as jaded as a thousand belly-rubbed green buddhas at disney world yet he smiles so big and thoughtful when i say something idealistic. he lets himself believe in it for 3 seconds and then says "isn't it pretty to think so?" quoting hemingway. i think he's trying to start over where relationships went wrong for him and he's a little nurtured by the newness, the awe, i feel.

so everything we do or will do feels like sad memories. on our third date we went to this deserted beach with fallen and stripped trees lining the shore. he's a photographer and had 3 different cameras with him. one was a polaroid. the bright sun overdeveloped the shots we took, so they looked faded. sitting on the back of his car, letting our feet drip dry, i looked through the pictures and said "they already look like memories."

\*

sorry to go on, writing is a way of extracting thoughts and making sense of things for me. this was probably a little too personal, especially since i haven't heard anything back from you to gauge what boundaries i should follow, but e-mail doesn't have much consequence if it isn't printed. it can get lost in transmission, deleted, or evaporate in some virus, like faulty prayers.

\*

Why is it sometimes life is too fake for fiction?

\*

"thpppppp"—that sigh horses and small children make. i'm bored. i don't wanna clean my room or do spanish make-up work. i feel very young today. i shopped for prom dresses and later described the cuts of the dresses according to disney princess movies. i'm debating on sleeveless snow-white or a lavender cinderella. yesterday, a 27-year-old guy asked me for my number and i said no. my shoes from 5 years ago still fit. for dinner, i had cookies and ice cream.

\*

across the street a man is pushing his granddaughter's red and yellow plastic car up and down the sidewalk and they're both laughing hysterically. he stopped to sit down and now she's checking her playschool wheels for a flat.

i paused and looked out the window because i wanted the "correct" words to describe my desperateness in writing. i do write. i suppose i mean my desperateness to write better. i want to have beautiful moments like the one across the street to be happening forever in a book somewhere. moments people forget to see, details i'm blessed with, the inexpressible grappled with, the meaning i can put into my neighbor's sea oat hedge, little things, i want available to others the way only i can see it. so i'm not sure if i am trying to convince you of my vision, or my words.

CHARLES BAXTER

## Infectious Reading

The Minneapolis Public Library in the 1950s stood on
Hennepin Avenue near Tenth, just across from Gmitro's
Ham'n'Eggs and within sight of the Orpheum Theater. The
place *looked* like a monument: pleasingly solemn, venerable,
five stories high, a pristine imperturbable eyesore. Constructed
of Minnesota red sandstone, it gave an impression of thick-
walled permanence—an atomic blast couldn't have blown it
away, I used to think. (The wrecker's ball finally got it.)

The first time I stepped inside, I went with my brother
Tom, whose idea it had been to show me the place. He parked
his Olds, valued at $120, two blocks away, and left it there
unlocked. At the library's main entrance, you had to step
down into a sort of well just below the sidewalk level to get in.
I loved the place immediately. It was overheated, as if for people who never exercised. The old books with their aging paper

made the interior smell like a bakery. After I stomped my snowy shoes in the foyer, my brother and I ambled past the checkout desks with their clicking Recordak machines making microfilm records of all the transactions, into a large room filled with blond-wood drawers. I had never seen a card catalogue that large before, and I found it hard to believe that each card represented a book in the library.

In the next room over, I carefully removed from the shelves a book about superheterodyne radios—my plans for adulthood included becoming a television and radio repairman who made house calls—and then we trudged up the circular stairs to the fourth floor, where there was a large and somewhat disorganized science exhibit on permanent display that included a stuffed lamprey, a rather cut-rate-looking mummy, and a model of the solar system. You'd go into a darkened room and gaze at the plaster-and-paste planets illuminated with ultraviolet light, and the starch in your shirt would start to glow, and you'd feel, standing there clutching your book about radio repair, just like an alien, weird and purple and stylish.

By the time I was thirteen I had perfected my reading posture: I had developed a method of slouching down in a chair so radically that my book, that fort of paper and glue and cloth, guarded my face. No one could see me when I was reading. They still can't. In those days I sat in chairs with my back down on the cushion, so that my torso was parallel to the floor. Only my head was propped up, and of course it was hidden behind the book. In the chair, I was a low rider. My mother thought that this method of reading would ruin my posture. She worried that I was becoming antisocial, that I would become one of those sad-looking run-down boys whom healthy girls would shun.

As it turned out, I had a large and eager appetite for trash.

Hemingway once claimed that his favorite book as a child was Jeffrey Farnol's *The Broad Highway*. Myself, I liked books about hot-air balloons and animals, but I wasn't really bookish until puberty arrived, and then I read art and garbage as consolation and stimulant, soaking it all up. In those days almost every novel seemed quite adequate. I liked them better, though, if they were voluptuously gloomy, or voluptuous *and* gloomy. *The Return of the Native* seemed like a perfect book to me, full of wounded stricken characters with all their eerie clumsiness and fatal calamities on display. In that novel, people are painted over with a red dye of sorrow. To quote a phrase used by the Quakers, the book spoke to my condition. You could also buy good novels in the paperback rack at the drugstore, and that's where I obtained Davis Grubb's *The Night of the Hunter* and J. R. Salamanca's *Lilith*, two books that made me want to be a writer. The first was about losing one's father and ending up in the hands of crazy people (my story exactly), and the second was about misplaced and probably crazy love, and both of them were written in a carefully wrought baroque-hypnotic style. They dazed me, those books.

I didn't want to become bookish and owlish, so I lifted weights and joined the wrestling team and pretended that the world as given to us was satisfactory, which, because the world *isn't* satisfactory, made me a hypocrite and unpredictably moody and a sort of manic-depressive athlete. All my efforts in the direction of the physical and material dimensions of my life seemed to fall short, but, armed with these other, more fugitive, psychic qualifications, I managed to become bookish anyway. I slouched in my chair and glowered and read all the time. I really don't know much about Davis Grubb (he died several years ago, and the only person I've ever met who knew him said that he looked rather like a large human frog), but I want to honor his memory here. Others can claim the truly great—Tolstoy and Shakespeare and Dante—as their child-hood and adolescent inspirations. I claim Grubb. I can't read his books anymore, but they were the first ones that success-fully spellbound me.

A ridiculous picture: a boy, lifting weights in the basement, takes breaks between sets of bench presses and biceps curls to read an American gothic-lyric novel by a man who looks like a frog. *The Night of the Hunter*, the novel he is reading, has at its center a luckless boy and the sister whom he must take care of and watch out for. My first novel, *First Light*, has at its center a brother and his sister, whom he thinks he must take care of and watch out for. Funny coincidence. You take your inspirations where you find them. About a year after *First Light* was pub-lished, I realized that I had embedded *The Night of the Hunter* inside it. That book infected me; it was infectious. These days, the sight of a kid, any kid, nose stuck in a book, is a reminder of that moody and solemn time of my life when I stepped out of one world—this one—into another, the parallel universe of literature, and felt that it welcomed me.

PATRICIA HAMPL

# Come Eat

Food was the potent center of my grandmother's life. Maybe the immense amount of time it took to prepare meals during most of her life accounted for her passion. Or it may have been her years of work in various kitchens on the hill and later, in the house of Justice Butler; after all, she was a professional. Much later, when she was dead and I went to Prague, I came to feel the motto I knew her by best—*Come eat*—was not, after all, a personal statement, but a racial one, the *cri de coeur* of Middle Europe.

Often, on Sundays, the entire family gathered for dinner at her house. Dinner was at 1 P.M. My grandmother would have preferred the meal to be at the old time of noon, but her children had moved their own Sunday dinner hour to the more fashionable (it was felt) 4 o'clock, so she compromised. Sunday breakfast was something my mother liked to do in a big way, so we arrived at my grandmother's hardly out of the reverie of waffles and orange rolls, before we were propped like rag dolls in front of a pork roast and sauerkraut, dumplings, hot buttered carrots, rye bread and rollikey, pickles and olives, apple pie and ice cream. And coffee.

Coffee was a food in that house, not a drink. I always begged for some because the magical man on the Hills Brothers can with his turban and long robe scattered with stars and his gold slippers with pointed toes, looked deeply happy as he drank from his bowl. The bowl itself reminded me of soup, Campbell's chicken noodle soup, my favorite food. The distinct adultness of coffee and the robed man with his deep-drinking pleasure made it clear why the grownups lingered so long at the table. The uncles smoked cigars then, and the aunts said, "Oh, those cigars."

My grandmother, when she served dinner, was a virtuoso hanging on the edge of her own ecstatic performance. She seemed dissatisfied, almost querulous until she had corralled everybody into their chairs around the table, which she tried to do the minute they got into the house. No cocktails, no hors d'oeuvres (pronounced, by some of the family, "Horse's ovaries"), just business. She was a little power crazed: she had us and, by God, we were going to eat. She went about it like a goose breeder forcing pellets down the gullets of those dumb birds.

She flew between her chair and the kitchen, always finding more this, extra that. She'd given you the *wrong* chicken breast the first time around; now she'd found the *right* one: eat it too, eat it fast, because after the chicken comes the rhubarb pie. Rhubarb pie with a thick slice of cheddar cheese that it was imperative every single person eat.

We had to eat fast because something was always out there in the kitchen panting and charging the gate, champing at the bit, some mound of rice or a Jell-O fruit salad or vegetable casserole or pie was out there, waiting to be let loose into the dining room.

She had the usual trite routines: the wheedlings, the silent pout ("What! You don't like my brussels sprouts? I thought you liked *my* brussels sprouts," versus your wife's/sister's/mother's. "I made that pie just for you," etc., etc.). But it was the way she tossed around the old cliches and the overused routines, mixing them up and dealing them out shamelessly, without irony, that made her a pro. She tended to peck at her own dinner. Her plate, piled with food, was a kind of stage prop, a mere bending to convention. She was a woman possessed by an idea, given over wholly to some phantasmagoria of food, a mirage of stuffing, a world where the endless chicken and the infinite lemon pie were united at last at the shore of the oceanic soup plate that her children and her children's children alone could drain . . . if only they would try.

She was there to bolster morale, to lead the troops, to give the sharp command should we falter on the way. The futility of saying no was supreme, and no one ever tried it. How could a son-in-law, already weakened near the point of imbecility by the once, twice, thrice charge to the barricades of pork and mashed potato, be expected to gather his feeble wit long enough to ignore the final call of his old commander when she sounded the alarm: "Pie, Fred?"

Just when it seemed as if the food-crazed world she had created was going to burst, that she had whipped and frothed us like a sack of boiled potatoes under her masher, just then she pulled it all together in one easeful stroke like the pro she was.

She stood in the kitchen doorway, her little round Napoleonic self sheathed in a cotton flowered pinafore apron, the table draped in its white lace cloth but spotted now with gravy and beet juice, the troops mumbling indistinctly as they waited at their posts for they knew not what. We looked up at her stupidly, weakly. She said nonchalantly, "Anyone want another piece of pie?" No, no more pie, somebody said. The rest of the rabble grunted along with him. She stood there with the coffeepot and laughed and said, "Good! Because there *isn't* any more pie."

No more pie. We'd eaten it all, we'd put away everything in that kitchen. We were exhausted and she, gambler hostess that she was (but it was her house she was playing), knew she could offer what didn't exist, knew us, knew what she'd wrought. There was a sense of her having won, won something. There were no divisions among us now, no adults, no children. Power left the second and third generations and returned to the source, the grandmother who reduced us to mutters by her art.

That wasn't the end of it. At 5 P.M. there was "lunch"—sandwiches and beer; the sandwiches were made from the leftovers (mysteriously renewable resources, those roasts). And at about 9 P.M. we were at the table again for coffee cake and coffee, the little man in his turban and his coffee ecstasy and his pointed shoes set on the kitchen table as my grandmother scooped out the coffee and dumped it into a big enamel pot with a crushed eggshell. By then everyone was alive and laughing again, the torpor gone. My grandfather had been inviting the men, one by one, into the kitchen during the afternoon where he silently (the austere version of memory—but he must have talked, must have said *something*) handed them jiggers of whiskey, and watched them put the shot down in one swallow. Then he handed them a beer, which they took out in the living room. I gathered that the *little* drink in the tiny glass shaped like a beer mug was some sort of antidote for the *big* drink of beer. He sat on the chair in the kitchen with a bottle of beer on the floor next to him and played his concertina, allowing society to form itself around him—while he lived he was the center—but not seeking it, not going into the living room. And not talking. He held to his music and the kindly, medicinal administration of whiskey.

By evening it seemed we could eat endlessly, as if we'd had some successful inoculation at dinner and could handle anything. I stayed in the kitchen after they all re-formed in the dining room at the table for coffee cake. I could hear them, but the little man in his starry yellow robe was on the table in the kitchen and I put my head down on the oilcloth very near the curled and delighted tips of his pointed shoes, and I slept. Whatever laughter there was, there was. But something sweet and starry was in the kitchen and I lay down beside it, my stomach full, warm, so safe I'll live the rest of my life off the fat of that vast family security.

JANE BROX

# Bread

Brot, bread, *pain, pane. Khoubz* in Arabic. Blessed, thanked for, kissed—like a child's hurt—if dropped. Sliced against one's woolen vest, sliced against the galvanized table top, or torn to sop up the last of a thin sauce. Once stale it was softened again in a salad of tomatoes and onions and oil, or broken into milky coffee for breakfast. Eaten with every meal; sometimes the meal was bread alone.

At the turn of the century in the central district of Lawrence, Massachusetts, there may have been as many varieties of bread as there were languages: a slack dough with olive oil added to it; caraway, butter, raisins; the loaves shaped into rounds or like slippers; braided, flat; the tops scored or sprinkled with seeds; glazed with milk to soften the crust, with egg white to give it a shine. But such variations are always smaller than the whole: flour, yeast, water, salt. When the corner bakeries were going full force, the air smelled simply of bread—yeasty, faintly sour—in the German neighborhood, the Irish, the Italian, the French Canadian, the Lebanese . . .

What could have lured so many different people here other than the rumor of work? Some, in their Italian villages, had heard rumors of money to be made in the needle trades. Some, like my father's parents, had already made tries in other American places—Olean, New York; Wheeling, West Virginia . . . When the work dried up, they followed news of more work, or went where there were others from their old country: so many starlings, wary, driven by innocent stirrings behind them.

Even with meager belongings—papers and change stowed in a breast pocket, a folded envelope of dried spices—when a family reached Lawrence, they'd find there wasn't enough space in the tenements for a world that had once spread across a valley floor. They strung up their laundry in the kitchen or between alleyways, and their chickens scratched at the basement floor near the coal bins. Goats, too, and pigs stowed in those tenements. Young children lit the kerosene lamps, started the stove, and waited for their parents to come home from the mills. And if, while waiting, a child looked out the alley window, instead of an immense and uninterrupted night, she'd see herself reflected in the glass.

Not much escaped and roamed freely other than the aroma of bread drifting into the households, here and gone and here again . . . *Brot*, bread, *pain, pane, khoubz*. The word alone in their native tongue. And theirs alone. Who among them believed *pane* and *khoubz* really meant the same thing?

The fires in the Syrian bakeries had to be white hot to form pockets in the flat loaves. The wood-fired ovens, fed with second-growth New England forests, must have burned far more wood in a year than many outlying farmhouses together. Farmers, if they could, would buy a woodlot just to keep themselves in fifteen cords a winter, and even then, the bedrooms were so cold come January their children's breath formed a fine rime on the hairs of the woolen blankets tucked beneath their chins.

Frost on the bakery windows turned to mist as the ovens heated up. Flour swirled in a slant of light and lined the creases of the baker's neck, salting his hair. He doused the work table with flour and kneaded the dough until it felt soft as an earlobe, then cut pieces off the mass and balanced them on the enamel scale. He flattened the pieces with the palm of his hand to make thin disks, which he slipped into the oven. In the intense heat of the fires the loaves puffed up, hollow in the center. Once out of the ovens they collapsed as they cooled, and he wrapped the bread in towels or muslin to keep it soft enough to fold around an olive or fresh cheese or a slice of cooked lamb.

By the early 1960s, when my mother made her trips to the bakery, the ovens were heated with gas or electricity and the bread was kneaded with a dough hook in an oversized steel mixer. And now the bread moves through the ovens on conveyor belts. The children of immigrants are at ease with English, and name their bread with adjectives: Irish soda, Syrian, Italian, Jewish rye . . . My mother used to buy a dozen plain loaves of Syrian bread, and one loaf each of fancier flatbreads, baked in cooler ovens, still eaten mostly by Syrians and Lebanese alone, and called by their old names: *simsim* and *zaatar*.

*Simsim* means sesame, a bread sweet enough to love right away. Its top is spread with seeds and drenched in a sugar syrup that's been flavored and scented with rose water. Mild and assuaging, it perfumes your mouth with its sweetness, and leaves a sticky mess on your hands and lips. Syrup pools on the plate.

*Zaatar* is topped with sumac. The dried red berries are crushed fine and mixed with olive oil, thyme, and oregano. Oil stains the waxed white bakery paper it's wrapped in, the spices and dried herb leaves on top are black from the baking. Dark as good earth, the taste of earth. Sumac, thyme, and oregano—used sparingly elsewhere—are used in abundance on *zaatar*. One strong flavor on top of another, acid compounded by bitter, the oil binding but not subduing them. It smells stronger than the yeast itself, and the air is full of its scent long after it's finished baking. Though there's no one in our family who doesn't love its rough flavor, *zaatar* is a long-acquired taste, and I don't see it traveling much farther than the Arabic language has in this valley: a Mass for the dead, the old folks talking among themselves. What few words we speak anymore we pronounce softly.

We saved plain loaves of Syrian bread for our meals, but we always ate *simsim* and *zaatar* as soon as my mother returned from the bakery. She'd cut a loaf of each into thin wedges, and we'd stand in the kitchen, leaning against the counters, eating *simsim* then *zaatar*, astringent *zaatar* then mollifying *simsim*, savoring one flavor even as we were thinking of the next, the wedges disappearing. I was never able to decide which I wanted to end with: the one almost too sweet, the other too pungent to translate.

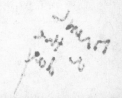

KELLY CUNNANE

# Clip from a Winter Diary

In the middle of the morning, she makes slices of herb bread with melted cheese. When they fuss, all day she cuts small squares and hands them to the complaining mouths. Later, she finds black cheese stuck in the rug, on the couch, but she has given, and that is all they want, although she knows it is not food they desire. Sometimes she gives out a story, and they huddle next to her and put her arm around them and fight about who has the most of her body next to them. The four of them are a corral, a fence within which she moves. She may run but not too far or fast. She may do whatever she wishes but inside the fence of them. The movement of them and the way they appear draws her toward them. She offers hot chocolate, a bubble bath, and they bound at her, squeeze her, and she turns on the TV and they disappear into its living color.

With snow on the ground, there is hope, and she bundles

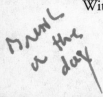

them and goes out into the pinched whiteness, its scrunch, scrunch. The noise of them dissipates and falls powdery off the branches of evergreens. She tucks the baby in a box with a blanket, so that only his round eyes show, and tugs him around and around and around the yard, her back hot and her cheeks burning. Anything that requires her mind can only occur in small, indecent intervals. Her body carries on with sweeping, crying, bursting out in laughter, and bends 100 times a day toward a toy, a child, mechanically, rhythmically. The computer, house building plans, articles to write, lie untended, five minutes here, twenty there. The snow and the sleigh bring her to life, and the moon comes up over the trees and when she lifts the baby from the box, he is still warm.

*Build in ambiguity*

# Missing

I miss my grandparents. My grandpa always wore a short-sleeved white shirt and a tie, even for our birthday parties, as if we were very important people. I was a star walking around town with him; he knew someone every half block, and introduced me like a celebrity. "AnnMarie's daughter," he would say. "Family is all that matters." He would have bingo parties for his grandchildren—we were in high school!—pennies for prizes, and each with our own snack of chips and dip on a Styrofoam meat tray. And every one of us came, just because he wanted us to. The times we misbehaved he called us "fresh." One time I decorated the dining room for his birthday. He was so pleased; he gave me rosary beads. They are in my underwear drawer right now. For his seventy-fifth birthday I made a cake with enough tiers to hold seventy-five candles. I wanted him to know I loved him. I have never felt so selfless again, ever. But now that I remember it, I am missing it. I know it is what would make me happiest, if I could love so selflessly again. . . .

My grandmother used to give my mother her bath when she was a baby, bundle her up, and then put my mom for a nap on the porch while she worked inside. I want to live in that world. Watching the news with my grandma was distracting, full of "tut tut" and "tsk tsk." The things people did, like taking something that was not theirs, amazed her. I am hardly ever amazed. Before she was married, she walked home from work at night alone, and all she could hear was the tapping of her shoes. She said she felt safe in the dark. Not me. She did all the caring and housekeeping for her family in a dress, with heels and stockings.

When I had to tell my grandparents that I was pregnant (even though I was not married) I don't remember them even blinking. Their faith in me was absolute. "She said she's pregnant," my grandma said. My grandpa said, "I know. You'll be okay. You'll do the right thing." Oh. And I was okay. I miss that.

KATHLEEN NORRIS

## At Last, Her Laundry's Done

Laundry seems to have an almost religious importance for many women. We groan about the drudgery but seldom talk about the secret pleasure we feel at being able to make dirty things clean, especially the clothes of our loved ones, which possess an intimacy all their own. Laundry is one of the very few tasks in life that offers instant results, and this is nothing to sneer at. It's also democratic; everyone has to do it, or figure out a way to get it done. When I picture Honolulu's Chinatown, circa 1960, which I passed through daily on a school bus, what I smell is the open-air fish market, but what I see are the signs, mysterious to me then, that read "Taxi Dance Hall: Girls Wanted," and all the colorful laundry strung up between tenements. There was never a day without it. In any city slum, it's laundry—neat lines of babies' T-shirts, kids' underwear and jeans—that announces that families live here, and that someone cares. For some people, laundry seems to satisfy a need for ritual. A television commentator with a hectic schedule once told me that the best, most contemplative part of his day was early morning, a time he set aside for laundering and ironing his shirts.

My images of laundry abound. One that I've never seen but love to imagine is that of Benedictine nuns in the Dakotas, in the days before Vatican II, when many of them worked in elementary schools, beating their black serge habits on snowbanks to get the dust out. They tell me that the snow was good for removing stains. I picture the small clothesline that a friend has put up in her penthouse garden in Manhattan. For her, laundry is a triumph of hope over experience. "I grew up in the suburbs," she explains, "and my mother hung clothes on the line. This is not ideal," she admits, "but on a nice windy day, the soot doesn't fall."

Of course an attachment to laundry can be pathetic, even pathological, in a woman who feels that it's one of the few areas in her life over which she has control. More often, though, it's an affectionate throwback to the world of our mothers and grandmothers. We may be businesswomen or professors, but it's hard to shake that urge to do laundry "the right way," just like Mama did. The sense that "laundry must not be done casually," as an arts administrator once told me, is something that seems lost on most men. She and her husband had reached an armed truce: he could do his own laundry but was to leave hers alone. She had grown tired of picking lint from his red sweatpants off her good blouses.

Many women have a "system" that is not to be trifled with. "You're hanging the underwear wrong" I was solemnly informed by a woman minister one day as we rushed to get her laundry on the line so that we could get to a meeting. She had a Master of Divinity degree from Princeton Seminary, but that's not where she learned that only a slouch would dare to use a dryer on a fine, windy summer day such as this in Lemmon, South Dakota, or that the fact was so obvious it could remain unspoken between us. She relegated me to the simple stuff, pillowcases and towels, but she kept an eye on me.

At St. John's we had been housed in a block of small, elegant, but very livable apartments designed by Marcel Breuer, and clotheslines were not permitted. The great architect found them "tacky," we were told, and visually distracting. It is good to be home, where I can hang clothes and air bedding on the line, and be as tacky as I like. I come by attachment to laundry honestly. One of my first visual memories is of my mother pulling clothes from the sky; she had a line on a pulley that ran from a window in our row house near the naval gunnery in Washington, D.C. These days, my mother lives in a neighborhood in Honolulu where her backyard clothesline is something of a scandal. But she's a Plainswoman at heart, and a clothesline is simple necessity.

Living in the house where she grew up, I've become pleasantly haunted by laundry. I'm grateful that I no longer have to pull clothes through a wringer, as my grandmother did for years. Her bottles of bluing gather dust in the basement; I haven't used them, but can't throw them out. But, like her, I wouldn't dream of using the electric dryer unless I have to. In March or April I begin to long for the day when I can hang clothes on the line again. Our winters are so long and severe in western South Dakota that we bank on the slightest summer joys; the scent of clothes dried out of doors, the sweet smell of sun on them.

I must be vigilant; sudden thunderstorms march across the prairie in late afternoon, making a mockery of clothes hung out to dry. Our winds can be so strong that clothes go flying. And during times of drought, there is sometimes so much dust in the air that line drying is impractical. Old-timers who recall the "Dirty Thirties" speak of seeing grasshoppers eat clothes right off the line, a sight I never hope to see, although I've thought about it in the springs and summers when we've waited months for rain.

My youngest sister once had a dream about a tornado that seemed an astute portrait of our parents: as the storm approached, Dad wandered off to get a better look at the twister and Mom ran to get the clothes off the line. I recall running into my clergy friend one evening at a church supper. She'd been frantically busy with meetings all day and the next night would be conducting a wedding rehearsal. News of a death in the congregation meant that she now also had a funeral to prepare for, and this led us to talk of epitaphs. "I know what I want on my tombstone," she said. "At last, her laundry's done."

KATHLEEN CAIN

# Asparagus

In the declining part of the year, as I walk along an unpaved road cut out of red earth, I pass a bush of wild asparagus. Its ferny branches reach nearly to my shoulders. The birds and animals that live along the road—scrub jays and robins, larks and swallows, a family of skunks, a small herd of deer, a solitary coyote whose tracks and scat I find each time I walk through these fields—have taken all but five of its red berries. I examine them closely, the way a child would. Their tops are capped with small corn-colored husks, shaped like five-pointed stars that have split open and then dried as the berries grew.

The berries have such depth of color that in eastern Europe perhaps, maybe in the Czech Republic or in Slovenia, I think the women would surely have created from the sight of them beautiful patterns or designs worked into the hem of a skirt, the edge of a bowl, the border of a painting, or the edge of a shawl. But whatever images women in distant countries might have gathered are not my recollections: only my imaginations. For me, the asparagus plant evokes a voice, a face, a time, a place. I grow smaller along the path until I am a child again, little more than three years old. I have some language of my own, but not much. A few words that I know and respond to, or can say in order.

I have to sort and store my world in sound, color, movement, shape. The voice I hear is—as I know now but did not then—that of a woman over whom death has already cast a closed net. Yet the sound of her voice in my memory is like a quiet tide coming in. Deep. Soft. Certain.

After more than forty years, I can still hear the sound of my own laughter in my grandmother's garden. I can hear the slow deep echo of her laughter as she kneels beside me, tickling my bare arms with the feathery leaves. She likes this, my laughter, and tickles me even more with the long delicate branches. But not too much. She doesn't tickle me too much, not unmercifully the way my father and my cousins do, or the big kids who live across the street.

It is quiet and cool in the garden this late Sunday afternoon. I know it is Sunday, even though I don't understand just how I know that, or remember the word for that day yet, or much about the way time moves. Perhaps it is only a looking-back kind of knowing, or maybe a knowing by sensation, because I do know it—by sight and sound of place—that this is where my family often comes on Sunday, to my grandmother's house. And that this is where I go with her, into the garden and into the chicken yard to help her. The earth is dark and wet, shaded by trees this time of day. Not the apricot trees because they are too small and on the other side of the house, but the big trees in the front yard that I don't know the name of, the ones that make dark spots on my grandmother's dress and on my skin when we stand beneath them together while she holds me in her arms and my father takes a picture of us.

I reach toward the red berries and my grandmother's voice, not alarmed, tells me not to eat them. Then she asks me if those little red berries don't look like they're on a Christmas tree. Christmas. That time is very far away. This is July, she says. I remember these certain words: *July garden Christmas tree asparagus*. And the red berries, which have a magic of their own, that don't need words to carry them forward out of memory. Magical red berries in the middle of my grandmother's quiet shadowed garden.

Maybe that was the day I learned about wishing. I don't remember whatever talk continued in the garden. I only remember that it was safe and full of love, for it can be evoked at the sight of a wild asparagus bush gone by at the side of a road made of red earth more than five hundred miles and forty years away from the end of that Sunday afternoon. My grandmother has been dead for those forty years. I grew into a woman myself long ago. The simplest act, even the memory of it, brings such simple peace. Beautiful and delicate and strong, like the asparagus plant itself, working such wonders from beneath the cold dark soil.

CYNTHIA OZICK

# Existing Things

First inkling. If I were to go back and back—*really* back, to earliest consciousness—I think it would be mica. Not the prophet Micah, who tells us that our human task is to do justly, and to love mercy, and to walk humbly with our God; but that other still more humble mica—those tiny glints of isinglass that catch the sun and prickle upward from the pavement like shards of star-stuff. Sidewalks nowadays seem inert, as if cement has rid itself forever of bright sprinklings and stippled spangles. But the pavement I am thinking of belongs to long ago, and runs narrowly between the tall weeds of empty lots, lots that shelter shiny green snakes.

The lots are empty because no one builds on them. It is the middle of the summer in the middle of the Depression, childhood's longest hour. I am alone under a slow molasses sun, staring at the little chips of light flashing at my feet.

Up and down the whole length of the street there is no one, not a single grownup, and certainly, in that sparse time, no other child. There is only myself and these hypnotic sema-phores signaling eeriness out of the ground. But no, up the block a little way, a baby carriage is entrusted to the idle afternoon, with a baby left to sleep, all by itself, under white netting.

If you are five years old, loitering in a syrup of sunheat, gazing at the silver-white mica-eyes in the pavement, you will all at once be besieged by a strangeness: the strangeness of understanding, for the very first time, that you are really alive, and that the world is really true; and the strangeness will divide into a river of wonderings.

Here is what I wondered then, among the mica-eyes:

I wondered what it would be like to become, for just one moment, every kind of animal there is in the world. Even, I thought, a snake.

I wondered what it would be like to know all the lan-guages in the world.

I wondered what it would be like to be that baby under the white netting.

I wondered why, when I looked straight into the sun, I saw a pure circle.

I wondered why my shadow had a shape that was me, but nothing else; why my shadow, which was almost like a mirror, was not a mirror.

I wondered why I was thinking these things; I wondered what wondering was, and why it was spooky, and also secretly sweet, and amazingly *interesting*. Wondering felt akin to love—an uncanny sort of love, not like loving your mother or father or grandmother, but something curiously and thrillingly other. Something that shone up out of the mica-eyes.

Decades later, I discovered in Wordsworth's *Prelude* what it was:

> *. . . those hallowed and pure motions of the sense*
> *Which seem, in their simplicity, to own*
> *An intellectual charm;*
> *. . . those first-born affinities that fit*
> *Our new existence to existing things.*

And those existing things are *all* things, everything the mammal senses know, everything the human mind constructs (temples or equations), the unheard poetry on the hidden side of the round earth, the great thirsts everywhere, the wonderings past wonderings.

First inkling, bridging our new existence to existing things. Can one begin with mica in the pavement and learn the prophet Micah's meaning?

KATHLEEN DEAN MOORE

# The McKenzie River

We advanced along the McKenzie River Trail with the efficiency of inventory clerks. Brown to purple flowers, heart-shaped leaves: *wild ginger*. Leaning, leafy stems, dense cluster of white flowers: *false Solomon's seal*. Three broad fan-shaped leaflets: *vanilla leaf*. The deer fern we knew, but a pale tattery fern stymied us. *Plants of the Pacific Northwest* said it might be a lady fern, easily confused with wood fern, page 26. Page 26 said it may be a wood fern, but check for sori that are crescent-shaped, rather than round. We trooped back down the trail to check the sori. There were none: a defective fern.

Single bell-like flower under each leaf: *twisted stalk*. Heart-shaped flowers in nodding clusters: *Pacific bleedinghearts*. *Maiden-hair fern. Monkey flower.*

I learned most of these names walking forest trails with my father, who was a taxonomist. Taxonomy, from the Greek word *nomos*, a rational principle, *taxare*, to rate, to place a value on, to assess, to call to account. In the field, my father carried a metal cylinder on a strap hung over his shoulder. A narrow, hinged door opened along its length. Whenever he found a plant that interested him, he cut it off at the soil, laid it carefully inside the cylinder, and shut the little door. At home, he spread newspaper on the kitchen table and laid out all the plants side by side. With a hand lens and a pair of tweezers, he dismembered each flower, separating all the petals, pulling open the tiny ovaries, following the paired steps in a dichotomous key. Once he had identified a plant, he wrote genus, species, date, and location on a sheet of newspaper and pulled the newspaper up over the face of the flower. By the end of the evening, he had a stack on top of a wooden pallet: cardboard, blotting paper, newspaper, specimen, newspaper, blotting paper, cardboard. He topped the stack with another wooden pallet and, kneeling on the press, cinched it tight with two straps. After many years, my father had taught himself the name of every plant in the weed fields and beech-maple woods around our town.

When our children came into the world, we taught them the names of things. Richard Scarry's *Best Word Book Ever* was the first bible in our house. We sat four abreast on the couch with the big book spread across our laps, and we pointed at the pictures and said the names. *Bus, Car, Bicycle, Truck, Pencil, Crayon, Paper, Book.* Jonathan's eyes followed Erin's little pointer finger up and down, across the page, through the book, as she pronounced all the words in the world. At that time, teaching them words seemed like the most important thing parents could do for their children.

When Lewis and Clark came into the West, they had the job of naming everything they saw. They named the trees: For the lodgepole pine, they chose *Pinus contorta*, because the lodgepoles they saw were coastal trees, twisted and dwarfed by Pacific Ocean storms. They named the birds: Clark's nutcracker. Lewis' woodpecker. And later, scientists named wildflowers in their honor: for Meriwether Lewis, a pink flower that blooms close to the ground in high, dry desert gravel—*Lewisia rediviva*, Lewis come-back-to-life, bitterroot; for Captain Clark, farewell-to-spring, *Clarkia amoena*, an evening primrose, a fan of pink petals, each petal with a purple spot in the center. Lewis and Clark named each river as they floated downstream: "Passed a small creek on Stard., at the entrance of which Reubin Fields killed a large Panther. We called the creek after that animal Panther Creek. The day before, found the river much crouded with islands both large and small and passed a small creek on Stard. side which we called birth Creek," because it was Captain Clark's birthday.

We have played the same game on our own river trips, landing on a gravel bar thick with willows and piles of mud-washed logs. We name the high places first, and then the low, hidden places. And then we conduct each other on guided tours, telling the names. By this ritual, the island belongs to us. We own Anniversary Island with Picnic Point and Dead Duck Beach. We own Family Island, canoeing out to reclaim it every summer when it emerges from spring floods, with new bays and logjams in need of names. We own our farm, not because of the mortgage, but because we have walked the land together and named the Oak Knoll, the Ash Swale, Turtle Point, Winter Creek, the North Hill pasture, and, above the railroad tracks, the Magic Forest. My father named the Magic Forest on his last visit west, when even his hand lens couldn't bring flowers into focus, and the plants confused him, so far from home.

———

Children bring their dolls to life by giving them names. Names transform animals into family members. In some religions, nobody can have eternal life—not even tiny babies—until they have been baptized, given a name. In a single word—*ilira*—the Inuit people bring to tangible life the awe and fear that possess them when they see a polar bear approaching across the ice; in another word—*kappia*—they name the apprehension that seizes them when they cross thin sea ice. In Genesis, all the parts of the universe are drawn out of fluid chaos by their names. "God called the dry land Earth, and the waters that were gathered together he called Seas." To be is to be named.

Yet no one is allowed to know God's name. He is called *yhwh*, a word without vowels, an obvious fake, a name that does not name. It is an issue, clearly, of disproportionate power. The power to name is the power to create, and the power to destroy.

Truck drivers call their CB nicknames *handles*, and this seems right. A handle gives leverage. Last year, a police officer leaned against the driver's side of my van. He wore reflective glasses that revealed my face, not his. "May I see some identification, please?" as I surrendered my driver's license, giving my identity over to the policeman. On the other side of the earth, Soviet citizens used to tell each other this joke: "I will describe to you the happiest day of my life. A knock came at the door of my apartment, and I opened the door to two men in trench coats. 'Is your name Ivano?' one said. 'No,' I said, 'he lives upstairs.'"

On duff under an uprooted fir, we found a slime mold, a bright yellow hauck of phlegm. When the kids poked at it with pine needles, every part they poked turned to water and disappeared. The slime mold defies classification and so defies naming. It isn't a plant because it moves around under its own power. And it isn't exactly an animal. After trying for decades to pin it down, taxonomists put the slime mold in its own kingdom—*Protista*, none of the above.

I wonder what it would be like to go into a forest where nothing had a name. If there were no word for tree stumps, would they sink into the duff? It's possible: After all, earth without form is void. And if we started over, giving names, would any fact about the forest compel us to name the same units? Would we label trees? Or instead would we find a name for the unity of roots and soil and microorganisms? Or would we label only the gloss of light on leaves and the shapes of shadows on the bark? How would we act in a forest if there were no names for anything smaller than an ecosystem? How could we walk, if there were no way to talk about anything larger than a cell?

All along the McKenzie River Trail, there must be things we do not see, because they have no names. If we knew a word for the dark spaces between pebbles on the river bottom, if we had a name for the nests of dried grass deposited by floods high in riverside trees, if there were a word apiece for the smell of pines in the sunshine and in the shadows, we would walk a different trail.

CECILE GODING

# How to Tell One Bird
# from the Next

By what one eats, he said, or on the other hand, by what one won't ever eat. By whether one likes to feed in the daytime or at night. This then, as much as where one likes to sleep, whether high in the branches or skootched down in the weeds. By the shape and size of the nest, if there is a nest. By one's connection with our closest body of water, and to what degree that body of water is necessary, more necessary than anything we can ever imagine.

He being our next-door neighbor for twenty-odd years. Those years, especially, when I was nine and ten and eleven and twelve.

Because I have been thinking lately about how it started, all this writing down. Growing up in the South in the sixties, when did I begin to write, to list, to particularize what I saw and heard? What I remember is: it started with birds.

Everything I remember has a field and a bird and a hand in it. And the air is always smoky. For the field across the road from our house seems to be always burning; it is a man who always burns the field—down to its roots, so it can be planted in something new. Something like alfalfa or corn or millet. Sometimes a kind of grass, succeeded by plump Black Angus heifers lazily grazing, or someone else's pet horses—all of this contained by a double strand of electric wire invisible from our porch. If you jumped the ditch, dropped a fresh blade of grass on the wire, and waited, the blade would twitch once and then lie still, browning.

In some cases, he might say, the name might derive from nearby kin, or country of origin. Another thing: if there is a close, but earlier-named, relative; it's by this other we come up with the name; thus the adjective "lesser" tacked to the name. By why lesser—why? Well, he might answer, because in some-body's eye, the greater looks to be brighter, rarer, more finely feathered—in somebody's estimation at least—but only when held up to the uglier brother, you understand. But "lesser than," the lesser defining the greater—so much that there is no need to even write "greater." Unless one is really great, like a really great Great Flamingo. Understand?

He the closest thing to a parent besides my own, and—he being slightly older than my own—I am thinking lately that losing him might be a kind of rehearsal in a way. If anyone needed a rehearsal. If there is any way the loss of one's parents can be rehearsed. But if it can, he seems a good place to start, because he seemed to be there at the beginning of something important that was happening to me, and to many children, this lifetime fascination with the particularities of the physical world, and with our obsessive particularizing of it, the neces-sariness of such busyness.

On the other hand—he might just as well say to a child

like myself—"great" just might mean larger, as in the Great White Heron. Likewise, there's nothing wrong with the "common" part of a name. "Common" just means there were millions of them at one time, certain gulls, for one. The one we think of when we say the word "gull." But that's just part of how to tell one from the other. And this is just part of all he taught me.

In 1960, my parents rented his wife's old family home for fifty dollars; we moved out of town to save on rent. So the two backyards, mine and his, shared the same wild masses of azaleas. He slashed a gap through them, so we could walk back and forth from our house to their house. Our only relation, then, was our proximity. But that's just part of it. Because there were those years that I, Cecile, was the one he chose to follow him around. Before me, he chose my sister. And after me, my little brother. So it was the age, then. There was a particular range of years when this neighbor—old now, not then—took us under his wing!—one by one, and showed us his life. Or I should say, he showed us his life list, the names of all those—all the plovers and goatsuckers and wrens, all the finches and creepers and terns—that he had ever spotted and identified in his entire life up to that point. He wrote them down.

In his other life, he was a postman. We would spend whole days driving around the South trying to see a man about a bird; we strung mist nets in the woods and fields to catch them, band them, and let them go again; we sent in all the names and dates and where we caught them. Someone, somewhere, received our names and tracked the migrations of all these ethereal hosts. In this life, too, he was a postman, a sorter of silhouettes, of colors and chirps. Yes, I am sure now that part of it was the age.

For twenty-odd years, one of his peacocks called down our chimney, "afright, afright"—whenever the train sounded at the Lynch's Creek trestle. The peacock was usually common and green, but for a while, the peacock that called down our chimney was white. A flock of our neighbor's guinea fowl slept beneath my window of an evening. Startled from sleep among the leaves, they would stretch their naked necks out, calling "Copperhead, Copperhead." When you hold a bird in your hand, the birds in the azaleas holler "Not me, not me." When you hold a bird in your hand, she closes her eyes. Her feet are covered with a hornlike material, either orange or black.

My neighbor kept a bobwhite quail caged at the edge of the yard, just for the sound. I pictured a soldier in a German prison camp, sending coded messages through cupped hands, to me on the other side. I pictured a man of a certain age, dropping into that life, his parachute deflating, fatigues becoming part of flesh over the years.

When you throw out your mist nets, you start with what flies in first. So I start with a man in a field, with what a person can teach a child to whom he is in no way, shape, or form related. I might begin with the shapes of the head, the mouth, the throat. And with the single spot of red which can only be seen upside-down, so that the name might descend from the man who first noted down that single spot of red. I might begin with the definition of a body against the sky, at daybreak, in a blackwater swamp for example, glimpsed through the cypress, through a pair of inexpensive binoculars.

JAMAICA KINCAID

# Garden of Envy

I know gardeners well (or at least I think I do, for I am a gardener, too, but I experience gardening as an act of utter futility). I know their fickleness, I know their weakness for wanting in their own gardens the thing they have never seen before, or never possessed before, or saw in a garden (their friend's), something which they do not have and would like to have (though what they really like and envy—and especially that, envy—is the entire garden they are seeing, but as a disguise they focus on just one thing: the Mexican poppies, the giant butter burr, the extremely plump blooms of white, purple, black, pink, green, or the hellebores emerging from the cold, damp, and brown earth).

I would not be surprised if every gardener I asked had something definite that they liked or envied. Gardeners always have something they like intensely and in particular, right at the moment you engage them in the reality of the borders they cultivate, the space in the garden they occupy; at any moment, they like in particular this, or they like in particular that, nothing in front of them (that is, in the borders they cultivate, the space in the garden they occupy) is repulsive and fills them with hatred, or this thing would not be in front of them. They only love, and they only love in the moment; when the moment has passed, they love the memory of the moment, they love the memory of that particular plant or that particular bloom, but the plant of the bloom itself they have moved on from, they have left it behind for something else, something new, especially something from far away, and from so far away, a place where they will never live (occupy, cultivate; the Himalayas, just for example).

Of all the benefits that come from having endured childhood (for it is something to which we must submit, no matter how beautiful we find it, no matter how enjoyable it has been), certainly among them will be the garden and the desire to be involved with gardening. A gardener's grandmother will have grown such and such a rose, and the smell of that rose at dusk (for flowers always seem to be most fragrant at the end of the day, as if that, smelling, was the last thing to do before going to sleep), when the gardener was a child and walking in the grandmother's footsteps as she went about her business in her garden—the memory of that smell of the rose combined with the memory of that smell of the grandmother's skirt will forever inform and influence the life of the gardener, inside or outside the garden itself. And so in a conversation with such a person (a gardener), a sentence, a thought that goes something like this—"You know when I was such and such an age, I went to the market for a reason that is no longer of any particular interest to me, but it was there I saw for the first time something that I have never and can never forget"—floats out into the clear air, and the person from whom these words or this thought emanates is standing in front of you all bare and trembly, full of feeling, full of memory. Memory is a gardener's real palette; memory as it summons up the past, memory as it shapes the present, memory as it dictates the future.

I have never been able to grow *Meconopsis benticifolia* with success (it sits there, a green rosette of leaves looking at me, with no bloom. I look back at it myself, without a pleasing countenance), but the picture of it that I have in my mind, a picture made up of memory (I saw it some time ago), a picture made up of "to come" (the future, which is the opposite of remembering), is so intense that whatever happens between me and this plant will never satisfy the picture I have of it (the past remembered, the past to come). I first saw it (*Meconopsis benticifolia*) in Wayne Winterrowd's garden (a garden he shares with that other garden eminence Joe Eck), and I shall never see this plant (in flower or not, in the wild or cultivated) again without thinking of him (of them, really—he and Joe Eck) and saying to myself, it shall never look quite like this (the way I saw it in their garden), for in their garden it was itself and beyond comparison (whatever that should amount to right now, whatever that might ultimately turn out to be), and I will always want it to look that way, growing comfortably in the mountains of Vermont, so far away from the place to which it is endemic, so far away from the place in which it was natural, unnoticed, and so going about its own peculiar ways of perpetuating itself (perennial, biannual, monocarpic or not).

I first came to the garden with practicality in mind, a real beginning that would lead to a real end: where to get this, how to grow that. Where to get this was always nearby, a nursery was never too far away: how to grow that led me to acquire volume upon volume, books all with the same advice (likes shade, does not tolerate lime, needs staking), but in the end I came to know how to grow the things I like to grow through looking—at other people's gardens. I imagine they acquired knowledge of such things in much the same way—looking and looking at somebody else's garden.

But we who covet our neighbor's garden must finally return to our own with all its ups and downs, its disappointments, its rewards. We come to it with a blindness, plus a jumble of feelings that mere language (as far as I can see) seems inadequate to express, to define an attachment that is so ordinary: a plant, loved especially for something endemic to it (it cannot help its situation: it loves the wet, it loves the dry, it reminds the person seeing it of a wave or a waterfall or some event that contains so personal an experience such as, when my mother would not allow me to do something I particularly wanted to do, and in my misery I noticed that the frangipani tree was in bloom).

I shall never have the garden I have in my mind, but that for me is the joy of it; certain things can never be realized and so all the more reason to attempt them. A garden, no matter how good it is, must never completely satisfy. The world as we know it, after all, began in a very good garden, a completely satisfying garden—Paradise—but after a while the owner and the occupants wanted more.

M A R Y   O L I V E R

# At Herring Cove

The edge of the sea shines and glimmers. The tide rises and falls, on ordinary not on stormy days, about nine feet. The beach here is composed of sand and glacial drift; the many-colored pebbles of this drift have been well rounded by the water's unceasing, manipulative, glassy touch. In addition, all sorts of objects are carried here by the currents, by the galloping waves, and left as the sea on the outgoing tide tumbles back.

From one tide to the next, and from one year to the next, what do I find here?

Grapefruit, and orange peel, and onion sacks from the fishing boats; balloons of all colors, with ribbons dangling; beer cans, soft drink cans, plastic bags, plastic bottles, plastic bottle caps, feminine hygiene by-products, a few summers ago several hypodermic needles, the odd glove and the odd shoe, plastic glasses, old cigarette lighters, mustard bottles, plastic containers still holding the decomposing bodies of baitfish; fishhooks rusty or still shining, coils of fishline; balls of fishline, one with a razor-billed auk in death-grip.

Sea clams, razor clams, mussels holding on with their long beards to stones or each other; a very occasional old oyster and quahog shell; other shells in varying degrees of whiteness: drills, whelks, jingles, slippers, periwinkles, moon snails. Bones of fish, bodies of fish and of skates, pipefish, goosefish, jellyfish, dogfish, starfish, sand dabs; blues or parts of blues or the pink, satiny guts of blues; sand eels in the blackened seaweed, silver, and spackled with salt.

Dead harbor seal, dead gull, dead merganser, dead gannet with tiny ivory-colored lice crawling over its snowy head and around its aster-blue eyes. Dead dovekie in winter.

Once, on a summer morning at exact low tide, the skull of a dolphin at the edge of the water. Later the flanged backbone, tail bones, hip bones slide onto the sand and return no more to the gardens of the sea.

One set of car keys. One quarter, green and salt-pocked.

Egg case of the left-handed whelk, black egg cases of skates; sea lace, the sandy nests of the moon snail, not one without its break in the circle; once, after a windy night, a drenched sea mouse.

More gorgeous than anything the mind of man has yet or ever will imagine, a moth, *Hyalophora cecropia*, in the first morning of its long death. I think of Thoreau's description of one he found in the Concord woods: "it looked like a young emperor just donning the most splendid robes that ever emperor wore. . . ." The wings are six inches across, and no part of them is without an extraordinary elaboration of design—swirls, circles, and lines, brief and shaped like lightning. Upon its taut understructure, the wings are powdery and hairy, like the finest fur closely shorn. White and cream and black, and a silver-blue, wine red and rust red, a light brown here and a deeper brown elsewhere, not to speak of the snowy white of the body's cylinder, and the stripes of the body, and the red fringe of the body, and the rust-colored legs, and the black plumes of the antennae. Once it was the hungry green worm. Then it flew, through the bottleneck of the deepest sleep, through the nets of the wind, into the warm field. And now it is the bright trash of the past, its emptiness perfect, and terrible.

WILLIAM HEYEN

# The Host

I think of a friend's field study of a New Guinea weevil. He tells me that when the insect matures it rolls over to gather a pod of soil on its moist back. The soil eventually sprouts algaes, lichens, mosses, microscopic ferns, mushrooms. Mites and pinhead snails and tiny marauding slugs take up residence in this miniature jungle, this whole ecosystem that the weevil bears on its back for camouflage and, no doubt, for other benefits still mysteries to us. The host seems even to regulate the weather of this world, touching it to dew, sunning it, shading it. When the weevil dies, the world on its back absorbs it, recycles itself, keeps saying itself down through time like a work of the imagination.

# James Alan McPherson

---

# Kani Wa Kora Ni Nisete Ana O Horu
# (Crabs Dig Holes According to the Size
# of Their Shells)

---

There was a Christmas morning, that first year, when something of the outside world intruded into my fortress. I had put up a Christmas tree the evening before, and had given it all the lifelights—bulbs, a star, an angel, and gifts—that were immediately available to me in this house. You know, Kiyo, from the early winter you spent here, just how essential this season is to me. When I send Christmas gifts now to my friends there, I like to imagine them floating all over Tokyo, Osaka, Nara, Sendai, Chiba, filtering gently into the homes of my friends like warm winter snow. Nepher called me here on Christmas Day, about three years ago, after she had received her gift. She laughed and said, "Santa Claus must have gone crazy!" This is when she began calling me "Jim-*chan*." I will admit it. I am childish about the Christmas season. I was once invited to take an inkblot test, and was asked to report to the tester the first familiar shapes that came into focus. Out of all the possible combinations of dots that might have constituted buildings, airplanes, cars, the faces and bodies of women and men, I saw only a Christmas tree. Such, apparently, is the importance of this season for me. But on that morning, because I was alone as usual, my plan was to sleep right through Christmas Day, and I was sleeping when the telephone rang. When I answered it, someone said, "My name is Howard Morton. I'm your neighbor across the street. My wife and I have been watching your house. We see you come and go, once in a while. Now we're worried about you. Your Christmas tree lights have been on all night, and we thought that something had happened to cause you to not turn them off. Are you all right? If you need anything, remember my name is Howard Morton. M-O-R-T-O-N. My wife's name is Laurel. Our telephone number is in the book. Merry Christmas . . ."

Beyond a simple expression of the Christmas spirit, Kiyo, there were several other values encased in this call. There was frugality, wariness, and also compassion. I had noticed this man and his wife across the street, coming and going, a number of times. They were "white." They were, in terms of the long, hard path I had had to walk to this house, no more to me than "other." Besides, my own world, in those days, extended only as far as the mailbox beside my front door. I went back to bed. But later, many months later, I placed this man's call, in memory, beside the rescue offered by the two "brothers" in the passing truck, the two beer-bloated white men on the lonely road the other side of Cedar Rapids, back in the early fall. Both couples, the two in the truck and the two across the street, had offered me a lifeline. After much more thought, many more months later, I began to understand that both lifelines had been extended out of a value-

bank, an old, obscure value-bank rooted in the practical neces-
sities of frontier life. Something is owed to the stranger, *any
stranger*, who seems to be in trouble. This something owed is
impersonal, no more than a simple expression of good manners. It is an unconscious habit, not a passion. The Romans
called it *communitas*. Here the word for it is *neighboring*. In
your language, Kiyo, the comparable word is *giri*.

But back then, during that first freezing winter in my
soul, I just did not *care* to understand. Instead, I focused on
patrolling my own habits inside this house. I remained loyal to
the ritual base of my own mythology. I controlled, with even
greater gloating, my watchful and strict remotion from the
life, *the animal life*, outside my screened bedroom window.
Nights, in my bed, I still paid careful attention to owls hoot-
ing nonchalantly, and then screeching, and field mice and
squirrels crying like babies before they died. I watched, in the
mornings, the sun-touched clean white snow, and very often I
could see paw prints of raccoons, and the lighter imprints of
squirrels, etched into the otherwise pure, *idealistically pure*,
disguise crafted by a benign nature to hide the terrible evidence of how the processes of life, *both animal and human*,
went their way. It was always warm, inside that bed, and most
nights I would leave the window open, no matter how cold it
was outside, and invite the frigid air to drift through my
screen and touch my head, and overcome the heat inside the
room, so that under my blanket I could generate more, *much
more*, of my own personal, private, unshared warmth. In this
way, remotely self-sufficient, and gloating, I passed my first
winter in this haven of a house.

But in the early spring, when the snow had gone away,
and when the trees that were in the backyard I had never
explored were once again in bloom, despite all my elaborate
patrolling and precautions, and, mysteriously, in defiance of

my screen, one morning something managed to invade my fortress. I awakened to find it crawling on my skin, beneath the blanket, and then it hummed and fluttered and panicked. And then it gave me a vengeful sting in the ass. As always, all windows in the house, and even my bedroom door, were closed. My bedroom window was, as always, screened. It is still, these many years later, a profound mystery to me, a *koan*, just how a spring bumblebee had wormed its way into the very center of the sanctuary I had so carefully constructed around the very outsides of myself, against the magnetic field of outside life. Something was denying me *peace* because I had denied it range and *meaning*.

# Bobcats

**I.** A white sandy lane in moonlight. A shadow emerging from tall grass along the edge, twenty steps ahead, standing broadside now, long-legged in the lane. You stop. Silhouette of bobcat. When the cat turns away, he is so narrow that he all but disappears. You follow, your deer rifle slung over your shoulder, you and the bobcat silently down the road, the cat no more than a shadow of a branch on the moonlit sand. You do not see him ease off into the grass, but after a while you know that there is nothing in the lane up ahead.

II. Driving along an unpaved road through the Savannah River swamp. A hard rain has just stopped and lush foliage, a wall of green on both sides, sparkles in the morning sun. Up ahead a blurred commotion—something striking through the wall onto the grassy edge and darting back, too quick for you to tell just what. You stop, get out. A small rabbit in the wet grass, hind legs kicking weakly, and in the soft white hair at its throat two spots of red, surgical.

III. From the tree stand you could still see, out on the edge of the field, shining in the dusk, the white belly of the doe you shot forty-five minutes ago, but on the ground dead grass stands head-high. It has grown cold since the sun went down. You shoulder through the grass a good hundred steps and break out into the open. There lies the doe. And something else—a shadow coalesced, perched upon the ribcage. You stop but the shadow blends into the darkness, leaving behind, like the stink of cat, an odor of resentment.

# The Indian Dog

When I was growing up I lived in a pueblo in New Mexico. There one day I bought a dog. I was twelve years old, the bright autumn air was cold and delicious, and the dog was an unconscionable bargain at five dollars.

It was an Indian dog; that is, it belonged to a Navajo man who had come to celebrate the Feast of San Diego. It was one of two or three rangy animals following in the tracks of the man's covered wagon as he took leave of our village on his way home. Indian dogs are marvelously independent and resourceful, and they have an idea of themselves, I believe, as knights and philosophers.

The dog was not large, but neither was it small. It was one of those unremarkable creatures that one sees in every corner of the world, the common denominator of all its kind. But on that day—and to me—it was noble and brave and handsome.

It was full of resistance, and yet it was ready to return my deep, abiding love; I could see that. It needed only to make a certain adjustment in its lifestyle, to shift the focus of its vitality from one frame of reference to another. But I had to drag my dog from its previous owner by means of a rope. It was nearly strangled in the process, its bushy tail wagging happily all the while.

That night I secured my dog in the garage, where there was a warm clean pallet, wholesome food, and fresh water, and I bolted the door. And the next morning the dog was gone, as in my heart I knew it would be; I had read such a future in its eyes. It had squeezed through a vent, an opening much too small for it, or so I had thought. But as they say, where there is a will there is a way—and the Indian dog was possessed of one indomitable will.

I was crushed at the time, but strangely reconciled, too, as if I had perceived intuitively some absolute truth beyond all the billboards of illusion.

The Indian dog had done what it had to do, had behaved exactly as it must, had been true to itself and to the sun and moon. It knew its place in the scheme of things, and its place was precisely there, with its right destiny, in the tracks of the wagon. In my mind's eye I could see it at that very moment, miles away, plodding in the familiar shadows, panting easily with relief, after a bad night, contemplating the wonderful ways of man.

*Caveat emptor.* But from that experience I learned something about the heart's longing. It was a lesson worth many times five dollars.

# Desire

Is desire, then, a sort of shadow around everything? Whatever my sister had—in this case, the hit record "Trip to the Farm"—I, by definition, wanted, because it had attained this one quality: it was outside my consciousness. The moment I held it, my mind experienced it, so I no longer wanted it.

All week long my sister and I would think and talk about *Batman* or *Get Smart* or *The Addams Family*—whatever the show was that year—and on the night of the show we'd make sugar cookies and root beer floats, then set up TV trays; immediately after the show, we'd talk about how much we hated that it was over and what agony it was going to be to wait an entire week for it to be on again, whereas the show itself was usually only so-so, hard to remember, over before you knew it.

Senior year of high school my best friend and I, who were both virgins, had to spend at least one night a week hanging around the San Francisco Airport. Why? The dirty magazines they let us flip through at the newsstand, of course, and the sexy stewardesses tugging their luggage like dogs on a leash, but more than that it was everybody marching with such military urgency to their destinations, as if everywhere—everywhere in the world: Winnipeg, Tokyo, Milwaukee—were to be desired.

I admire the Boy Scout belt a friend of mine is wearing—I like the way it is a joke about uniformity at the same time it simply looks good—and when I ask where he got it, he says, to my astonishment, that it is his original Boy Scout belt: he still has it; he can still wear it; he is very skinny, stylish, good-looking. I never made it past the Cub Scouts and even in the Cubs failed to distinguish myself; slipknots and shiny shoes have never been very high priorities for me. But now I want a Boy Scout belt and think it will be easy. I stop in at a Boy Scout office, where I am told that BSA clothing and accessories can be purchased only by Scouts or troop leaders. I go so far as to schedule an interview for a troop leader position until, fearing accusations of pedophilia, I end the charade. Visits to several stores lead me to the boys' department of JCPenney, which carries Boy Scout uniforms in their catalogue and tells me I can order a belt. They call me when it comes in. I wear it once, maybe twice, with jeans, then toss it into the back of the closet.

JOHN ROSENTHAL

# One Afternoon

One afternoon in the late 1980s, while I was rummaging around in my basement in North Carolina, I came across the little red cardboard box that contained my first record collection. After all these years of being stored in damp basements and sweltering attics, it was intact but a little ragged at its edges, not unlike its owner who'd been through a couple of marriages and half a dozen love affairs. As I lifted the box off the shelf by its little red plastic handle, a small hinge gave way and a number of records spilled onto the basement floor. Kneeling down, I began to pick them up carefully as if they were relics, the bones of a forgotten saint once imbued with a radiant life. Here was Perry Como's "Don't Let the Stars Get in Your Eyes," a blur of scratches across its minutely grooved surface. For a fraction of a second I pictured little Dorothy Ewing, aged eleven, in a brown dress with yellow polka dots. I

was sure that I would love her forever. Of course. Even though
the record was ruined, I held it gently in my hand, making
sure my fingertips didn't touch its playing surface. And here
was Eddie Fisher's "Count Your Blessings." My brother, always
a nice guy, used to sing that when he was fifteen. Unplayable.
Warped. I thought to myself: there must have been a few years
when I left the lid open, I should have been more careful.
Reading the titles of the songs I used to sing thirty years ago, I
experienced a small whimsical shock. Was this the music that
introduced me to American popular culture—that giddy,
extroverted, crowd-pleasing, compellingly childish Dreamland
that for years offered me a place to hide from the more precise
claims of self?

Patti Page's "Doggie in the Window." I bought that?

A small voice in the back of my mind said, *Of course you
did. And you still remember all the lyrics.*

"The Ballad of Davy Crockett" by Bill Hayes. Bill Hayes?

Again the voice: *He also sang "The Ballad of James Dean,"
which you listened to for weeks.*

Ah, "Sixteen Tons." That was a good one.

*"One fist of iron, the other of steel"!*

"The Yellow Rose of Texas"??

*Easy, it was your favorite song.*

"Love and Marriage" by Frank Sinatra. Terrible, terrible.

*I agree, but you still sing it in the shower.*

As I picked up the 45 of "You're Wrong, All Wrong," sung
by the long-forgotten Eileen Rogers, I remembered how I
used to imagine myself bravely, even magnificently, enduring
the loss of love. The truth was, however, that once I entered
into the actual business of falling in love with girls, I quickly
lost all interest in sacrificing myself to an ideal devotion.
Ordinary love was hard enough; too hard most of the time,
actually. Nor did I ever imagine the horrors of jealousy that

waited for me in the near future, and which, on more than one occasion, reduced me to a subhuman state. It wasn't love that ended up dominating my life, but its pursuit.

Is it possible, I asked myself in the dim basement with its faint smell of mold and damp earth, that anybody else in the world collected such silly music with such single-minded devotion? Of course my question was rhetorical. There were thousands of us, musically damaged boys and girls who thrilled to those cascading violins and believed with all our little palpitating hearts in those grandiose, octave-jumping sentiments.

As I stood there thinking about the implausibility of things, "You're Wrong, All Wrong" slipped from my fingers and fell to the concrete floor. Landing directly on its edge, the 45 cracked. I picked it up quickly, thinking: "If I glue it together, it'll still play." But the record was gone, and for a second or two I felt stunned, as if I'd just received bad news. What news? What did I care about a stupid record I hadn't played in over thirty years? I didn't even have a 45 record-player to play it on. I tossed the little disc into a trash basket and put the cardboard box back on the shelf, closing its lid as tightly as possible.

KELLY SIMON

# Frank Sinatra's Gum

It was 1945 and Frankie, the Voice, was singing at the Paramount. Though I pretended to swoon at the mention of his name so I would fit in—a ploy that caused my father to lump me with "the rest of those drooling, moronic, autograph-hunting sheep"—secretly I did not adore him like the other girls in junior high did. Still, I knew if I could get something of his, they might include me in their cliques.

I liked that he was Sicilian as many of my father's friends and clients were. Sicilians ate spicy food, waved their arms around, argued in loud voices, and kissed and made up, unlike my mother who did none of these things except argue loudly and wave her arms around.

Even though his father was born in Austria and he, himself, was born in America, I thought of my father as Sicilian. He walked like the Sicilian men did—with his hands clasped behind his back. He kissed men on the lips and pinched their cheeks as I had seen Sicilians do. He was a pug like Frankie who—even though he was skinny and wore a bow tie—punched reporters when they got too close. Until my father married my mother he, too, used his fists to settle fights. When he was eighteen he knocked a boy out and when he tried to revive him, the boy just lay there on the sidewalk. Thinking he had killed him, my father skipped town. A month later, when he heard that the fellow was alive, he came back.

I took the train into New York the day that Frankie was to appear at the Paramount. Girls in bobby socks squealed and fainted as they swarmed the box office trying to get in. After standing in line for two hours, I learned that all the tickets were sold out. I had planned for this possibility and I ducked around to the stage door entrance and knocked. A man with a cauliflower nose stuck his head out.

"Yeah, what?"

"I'm a reporter for the Weequahic High News. I came to interview Mr. Sinatra."

"Who says?"

"I wrote him a letter last month," I lied.

"Wait here," he said, and closed the door.

Moments later, he came back. "He's in between shows. He says make it snappy."

I had thought things out to here, never expecting to get in. Now what? The man brought me to Frankie's dressing room. Frankie was sitting at a small table. He grinned when he saw me and suddenly it occurred to me, Frankie, the Voice, the Crooner, was grinning at me! I stood rooted to the spot, expecting to faint dead away like the shrieking, swooning girls outside who were carted off by the hundreds by the police. I waited to feel light-headed, for my knees to grow weak, but nothing happened.

Frankie pointed to a chair opposite him. I sat. He peeled the paper from a stick of Juicy Fruit—very slowly it seemed—crumpling the wrapping and compressing it between his thumb and index finger into a tiny ball the size of a pebble. He tossed it overhand at the wastebasket across the room.

"Missed," he said, as it hit the side and fell on the floor.

I wrote this in my notebook.

Looking directly into my eyes, he folded the gum in half then in half again and placed it on his tongue. I glimpsed the inside of his mouth lined with long almost-colored teeth that rested against the pink wetness of his cheeks. Past the stick of gum that lay upon his tongue like a tiny jelly roll I saw his uvula, pink and tremulous, whose flutter was, in a measure, responsible for his gift of song. I was mesmerized. Like one of those squealing, moronic sheep that my father so despised, I stared into the theater of his mouth at this small pendant of flesh, waiting for inspiration. Then the curtains of his lips closed and he grinned and cracked his gum.

"You got three questions."

I tried to think of something to say, but my mind was blank. I saw a *Herald Tribune* lying on the table next to him. "Congress declares that The Lone Ranger and Frank Sinatra are the prime instigators of juvenile delinquency in America," it read.

I took a deep breath. "Is it true you were the ringleader of a gang and your nickname was 'Angles'?"

Caught in mid-chew, his mouth remained open for a moment. Then it closed.

"That was a long time ago," he said.

I wrote this in my notebook.

"Is it true you were classified 4-F because of a punctured eardrum?"

He leaned his elbows on the table. His face was inches

from mine. His baby blues twinkled at me. I could smell the
Juicy Fruit on his breath.

"I would love to be over there defending my country but
someone has to stay home and mind the henhouse." He took
his gum from his mouth, parked it under the table and leaned
forward. "You got one more question." My hand under the
table worked his gum loose. Anyone could get an autograph,
but Frankie's gum!

I said, "Is it true you gave Ava Gardner a $10,000 emerald
necklace while you were married to Nancy Barbato?"

"The only present I ever gave Ava was a six-pack of Coke."

I wrote this in my notebook.

When he wasn't looking, I put his gum in my mouth. It
tasted chewed out, unsugary. In the hallway as I was leaving,
the man minding the door looked sidewise at me when I spit
it into the trash.

R<small>EBECCA</small> M<small>C</small>C<small>LANAHAN</small>

# Considering the Lilies

If God had wanted us to be nudists, we would have been born that way. That's what a woman's voice was saying, right there on the *Joe Pyne Show*. Thirty years later I remember her flustered reply. She had called in to register indignation at a nudist—clothed for the camera—who had been stating his case.

*

In the long stretch between wives, my brother dated women who, in his words, could wear clothes. Doesn't everyone wear clothes, I wondered, failing to see that the emphasis was on wear—an active verb, something a woman's body did to the clothes. He came dangerously close to falling in love with a secretary with whom he spent lunch hours, marveling as she modeled before the three-way mirrors of posh shops. She always left with a shopping bag full.

How can you afford it? he asked one day.

She smiled wryly, as if amused at the question. He recalls that her reply struck him like a sexual betrayal: I shoplift, of course. Don't tell me, after all this time, you haven't known.

\*

If you're a woman who doesn't wear clothes, you know it. There is always something amiss—off-toned stockings, a lining that grabs. You check yourself in the mirror, once, twice. Turn to the side, girdle your abdomen, rehearse a subtle smile. You think this moment will hold. Fifteen minutes into the party, the moment-before-the-mirror unravels. Something is amiss, you're not sure what. Something is not holding.

\*

In an early Woody Allen film, a poor and lovely girl sits opposite him at a table, her skin flawless as a petal. It's their first date, and she wears a hat with a small feather.

Nice hat, he says. I've seen them around, in those big bins.

She shakes her head, confused. She had hoped to please him.

Yes, I'm sure, he insists. Whole bins of them. All over the city.

\*

Somewhere in this city is a woman with my body and my taste in clothes. She can afford the taste. I shadow her, snatching up her discards a season after she steps out of them. Gently worn, the proprietor calls the clothes in her shop. She tells me there is a celebrity consignment store in Beverly Hills where women pay thousands of dollars for a dress that belonged to Liz or Barbra. The woman I am shadowing is client number sixty-eight. I don't know her name and don't wish to, but I would know her clothes anywhere. The proprietor watches as I enter. She says she can predict which jacket I will approach, which pair of slacks. I like to imagine the phantom woman. Does she shop in my grocery store? Has she passed me in the aisles and recognized herself in this stranger wearing her clothes?

*

My friend, a stylish gay man in his late seventies, has beautiful hands and always wears a bandanna at his neck. Twice a month we go to dinner. His eyes are shutters clicking on the most elegant man or woman in the restaurant. In his youth he was a fashion photographer.

They were exquisite, he recalls of the models from the 'forties. Simply exquisite.

He's arriving within the hour to pick me up. I search my closet. Once, years ago, he complimented me: it was a plain black dress with large lapels, and I'd paid too much for it. I wore it with my favorite necklace, a loop of pearls my father had given me when I turned eighteen.

My friend said, You should see yourself in this light, with your head turned just so.

*

We wear what we wore when we were happiest, the fashion consultant says. The boardwalk at Atlantic City is littered with the past—cigarette-leg capris on aging tanned women, lacquered bouffants under pastel nets. In the upscale mall of my city, young wives shop for pinafore-bibbed dresses that tie in the back. From birth to death, and all stations between, we are swaddled and bound. Even the Bible has a dress code. Ashes and sackcloth for mourning, white linen for angels and the newly resurrected. Rich men wear soft clothing, Job wears worms on his flesh. You can spot a virtuous woman by the purple silk, an enemy by his sheepish clothing. Promises and threats abound: I will clothe you in riches and honor. Then, in your lamentation, rend and tear what covers you.

*

Here, my father would say, handing my mother some bills. Buy yourself something. You're worth it. Splurge. My father loved beautiful clothes, and wanted a wife who loved them too. While he was stationed in Japan, he commissioned a tailor to fashion two suits for my mother. One was blue silk, the other boiled wool the color of milk chocolate. Both were lined in maroon taffeta on which her initials were stitched in gold thread.

My mother always took the money he offered. Hours later, she returned with skirts for her daughters, trousers for her sons, sometimes a bolt of stiff fabric from which she would sew curtains, tablecloths, house dresses.

*

We put an outfit on layaway, my best friend wrote. It was 1963 and the news was important enough to warrant the 3,000-mile mail route from the town our family had recently left. She enclosed intricate sketches of an olive-green three-piece ensemble, exclaiming over its versatility, how it would carry her through several seasons. Reading the letter, I remembered all the Saturdays I'd walked to the department store with her, visiting an item that would be released after the first or fifteenth of the month, when her widowed mother got paid. I was small then, so I didn't notice—until many years later—how small their house was. Her mother was small, too, and worked long hours to buy the clothes her daughter coveted.

*

The day shift is ending. Three women shuffle from the mill's gray exterior, wearing names and younger faces on identification badges. Shoulder bags, weighted with the day's needs, hang nearly to their knees. One woman has tucked stretch pants into high-heeled boots. One matches all over. The third wears a beaded belt cinched so tight that her stomach blooms beneath and above. Their efforts make me sad. How many bins have I rummaged with these women? In dreams we tumble together in huge bargain barrels, smothered in ginghams, tweeds, tartan plaids. We dive deep, searching for logos. I have a butcher knife and I'm thinking when I find a label that matters I will slash it into shreds—This one's for you, Pierre, and for you, Donna— but it's too late, they've arrived ahead of us again, vandalizing their names as if ashamed to be linked with us: seconds, slightly irregular, imperfect. We crawl from the bin, grasping our prizes.

*

Laura Ashley, the comedian says. For the woman whose goal in life is to look like wallpaper.

*

The magazine photographer lights upon some woman on the street, a school teacher this time. She will appear in next month's issue, beneath the heading *Fashion Don'ts*, her eyes x'ed out as if she's been caught in a crime beyond belief. The blindfold is a gift, the kindness of an executioner who cancels out the prisoner's last view: *She never knew what hit her.*

*

Condemned girls, under SS guard, spent their last days ripping sleeves off coats and replacing them with sleeves of different colors. They painted the back of each coat with a red bull's-eye for the marksman stationed above the electric fence. Some prisoners threw themselves against it. In the morning the girls tied belts around the ankles of the dead and dragged the bodies to the meadow. If a dress suited, if a pair of shoes fit, they took it.

*

If we were in the chemo ward, we would sadden or sympathize, but here in this uptown Bohemian restaurant, our young waitress is beautiful and admired, her white scalp visible, black hair bristling from each follicle. Fashion, I decide, is mostly context.

Stunning, says a middle-aged man seated with a forgettable woman at a nearby table. He can't take his eyes off the waitress.

Fashion also implies option, choice. The same runway frame a designer hangs dresses on, holds up the gown of the dying woman I visit each week. She sucks on ice chips, her cheekbones the kind that plump girls reading magazines would die for.

\*

In the dream I am standing with my dead mother before her closet, arguing about what she should wear for eternity. I suggest the blue silk with maroon lining. She pulls out a pair of paint-speckled dungarees.

Mother! I cry.

I don't see why it matters, she says. As long as it's comfortable.

\*

My friend, a middle-aged man recently divorced, tells me how simple it once seemed—how, as a young man, all he wanted was a woman who looked good in a suit. One afternoon thirty years into the marriage, his wife walked out of a dressing room *wearing* a suit. He was stunned to realize he not only possessed his desire, but had possessed it all these years. In the same moment, he realized it was not enough.

It was the saddest day of my life, he said.

\*

It's 1965, and I'm sharing a bed with my cousin the night before her wedding. She's eight years older, petite and boyish, still a virgin.

In the dark she says to the ceiling, I have the kind of body that only looks good naked. The tone is half lament, half expectation. For years she's been hiding beneath her clothes a lovely secret which is about to be spoken.

DIANA HUME GEORGE

# On Seat Belts, Cocaine Addiction, and the Germ Theory of Disease

I consented to accompany my mother on a short car trip to see relatives at a family reunion. Mom has always been a disaster-monger, a creator and celebrant of crisis, a firm believer in the germ theory not only of disease but of life, which come to much the same thing for her. She is sure I am going to get every conceivable disease this yeasty, critter-ridden life has to offer—and I'm going to deserve all of them. When I was in England for a while a few years ago, she sent me a news article about a cholera epidemic in Africa. Across the top she had printed in capital letters: SAVE IN CASE CHOLERA REACHES ENGLAND. When my son had a cold and Mom came with a prescription for him, she strapped on a surgical mask before she would leave her car. (She, too, is going to get every conceivable disease if she doesn't watch out—but she will not have deserved them.)

Nor are germs and viri the only things about which she is deathly concerned. Chief among her worries about this careless, too emotional, haphazard life she knows I lead are those that stem from active irresponsibility. During my thirties, she regularly sent me news clippings about the correlation between reproductive cancer and promiscuity. No matter that I had been in only one relationship for fifteen years at that time. She fears I'm a slut at heart.

In a classic case of thickheadedness, I answered honestly her questions about what kinds of experimenting I had ever done with drugs. When I went to college some of my friends consumed enough drugs to open pharmacies. All I really did was smoke marijuana occasionally at weekend gatherings, with the doors locked, the candles lit, and the nickel bag next to the toilet—this at a time when some people I knew were doing reefer on public streets. But I didn't have the sense to lie, and while the reaction wasn't immediate, Mom kept her counsel—she knew what she knew—and when the glossy mags started printing articles about the cocaine epidemic in the middle class, she called me and said she had something serious to discuss with me, and would I take the phone to a private place where no one could hear what I might say. Mom confided in a firm but loving voice that she knew about my cocaine addiction, and that she would be there to help me when I was ready to acknowledge it and save my life.

This is what comes of telling my mother the truth. I am dim about getting it through my head that I should lie to her. This is ironic, because one other thing my mother knows about me, and has known since I was a (difficult) child, is that I am a pathological liar. She can recite by heart every lie she caught me in when I was ten and twelve and fifteen, and she can also recite, with equal conviction, five times as many lies I never did tell that she is sure I did. *Pathological.* That's her word for it. All this is preamble to Mom's current campaign of love—for she tries to get me to see the errors of my ways only because, of course, she loves me. Mom has been running short on material as I enter my staid middle age, but she is an endlessly resourceful woman who does not need anything as paltry as facts on which to base her concerns.

Now, I have always worn my seat belt at almost all times when I am in a moving vehicle. Okay, not when I'm on a long car trip and need to sleep in the back of the van between driving shifts, but otherwise I'm in the front, swaddled in shoulder and lap belts. One time Mom asked me about my seatbelt habits, and I did it again—I am such a dumb bunny—and told her that while I wear my belt 99 percent of the time, I can't belt when I'm riding in the back bed. That did it. Well, she knew anyway. I'm the kind of person who has no regard for safety, no sense of responsibility toward those I would leave behind if I were to die in a car accident. For years she had inquired about it suspiciously, but my denials threw her off course a bit—until the family reunion.

I was ill for that trip. I got food poisoning just hours before we left, and although I had thrown up more times than is decent to recount, I was still nauseated. This trip was so important to Mom that I went anyway. I got in the back seat, and, knowing that it was a mistake, lay down and hoped I would not die. Some of the time, I hoped I would. All the way, Mom made judiciously spaced comments about the fact that while I was lying down, I was unbelted, and this was unsafe, and she had warned me what might happen, and this was her car, and she required passengers to belt, *ad* literal *nauseam*. But not even having to listen to this recurrent refrain could budge me, I was that sick.

It's been well over a year since that trip. In the interim, Mom has sent me clippings about seat belts and safety. She has spoken with my son about it on the side, trying to get him to turn in his law-breaking mother to the judge and jury consisting entirely of Grandma. During this year, I have of course continued to do what I always do—I wear my seat belt. I often belt up as I'm pulling out of a parking lot, and when Mom and I go to lunch, I have several times seen her standing near her car, squinting into the tinted windows of my car to see what she knows is there behind the glass—a woman thoroughly exposed to the dangers of the road, to other drivers even drunker than she often is; and this woman, this irresponsible daughter and not-any-better-than-she-should-be mother, is often probably so coked up that she will not know when to put on the brakes. She may well be dying of reproductive cancer brought on by rampant promiscuity, but is there any need to hasten her inevitable end—a sad one, indeed, but choices have consequences in this life—with unwarranted lawbreaking and complete lack of regard for the welfare of those who have a right to depend upon her, and never could? She knows what she knows.

As I write this, I am on vacation, sunning myself (read: laying a good base for skin cancer), and swimming in a sea of poisonous creatures who will bite me, if I'm sensible enough not to go out too deep and drown myself while I'm high. I call Mom dutifully, expensively, long distance, three times a week. During these conversations, Mom goes on about seat belts. She knows I did not wear them on the trip here. She knows I will not wear them on the trip back. She knows it is her duty to try to avert the coming disaster. I say to her that she cannot expect to suggest that I am a liar without my objecting to it now and then. She says I must be premenstrual, because it's clear that I am unable to speak reasonably about controversial subject matter. Very well, she will wait. She will not mention it again right now—she sees that I am overwrought. (I have

always been, in addition to "difficult," easily "overwrought.")
All of this is because she loves me. It really is.

A new campaign—or the renewal of an old one—is about
to replace seat belts. Recently my relationship of several years
changed from romance to friendship and I became partner-
less, a fact that did not escape my ever-vigilant mother. When
I went to a conference run by an old friend, Mom was on the
job immediately. Did I go to this workshop alone? Yes.
Mmmmm, she replied. And did I get together with my "old
friend"? Yes. I see, she said. And were you staying at the same
hotel? Yes, everyone was in the same hotel. And is he married?
Yes. And was his wife with him at this conference? No.
Mother came out with it. Had there been any hanky-panky
between us? No, Mother, of course not, he's an old friend.
Literally. He's almost seventy. She is also gearing up for the
upcoming visit of another friend, recently divorced. Am I
aware that Tom could have been with *anyone at all* since his
divorce? Mom, he's got a girlfriend, they're buying a house.
House, schmouse, am I aware that there are diseases out there?
Yes, Mother, I've actually heard that.

A few days after this talk, the phone rang again. On my
end, you'd have heard, "Thanks so much, Mom. Cereal? Cereal
what? What kind of cereal?" On her end, it went like this:
"Now I'm not *saying* you're actually *promiscuous*, dear. What
you do isn't that, it's, it's that thing that's got serial in it. You
know—serial—serial—what is it? Monogamy, that's right, it's
monogamy of a sort. Don't you think it's unfortunate that you
can't seem to make a relationship last?" Indeed. I tell my adult
daughter Kris. *You slut*, she says. We love that word. I sprinkle
monogamy on my cereal. We're going to create a cereal for
promiscuous middle-aged divorcees. We'll call it Slutty Charms.

KIMBERLY GORALL

# The End of Summer

It was one of those sticky August days. Supper was over, and I'd hurried through the dishes to pursue my backyard passion. During those long school-free months, my father, brother, and I played baseball with the neighbor boys' every evening till the sun slipped behind our willow tree.

I was in the outfield when my father called out that my mother wanted me in the house. I felt a pang of apprehension. In our family, you could be in trouble and not even know it.

I walked cautiously into the kitchen. As usual, my mother sat cross-legged at the table, a booklet of prayers and a mug of instant coffee in front of her, a tendril of cigarette smoke ascending from her hand. My older sister Donna was there too.

"Sit down. I want to talk to you," my mother said, not looking up.

I sat.

"You're almost in the fifth grade," she began. "You can't walk around like that without a shirt any more."

"But it's *hot* outside," I protested. "I'm dyin'!"

"Girls have to wear shirts."

"But boys don't!"

"That's boys. You're a girl."

"But it's not fair!" I argued, feeling the familiar sting of a double standard. Girls couldn't have footballs, slingshots or pitcher's mitts. Boys didn't have to cook or baby-sit or do the dishes. Girls couldn't wear pants to school, even in the winter. Boys could be secret agents and astronauts. Girls had children. Boys had fun.

"You have to wear a shirt, and I don't want any arguments."

"All the time?"

"That's right."

My mother shifted uncomfortably in her chair. I sensed there was more.

"Pretty soon you'll become a woman," she said, sounding cheerful, rehearsed.

Who cares, I thought, cringing. What was her point? I was missing the game.

I stared at her impatiently.

Finally she said weakly, "You'll bleed in here," pointing down to her lap.

Horrified, I began to cry.

"Good one, Mom," my sister chided, rolling her eyes.

"Oh . . . ," my mother moaned, her voice trailing off. Then she, too, started crying.

I stood up, grabbed my glove, and headed for the door.

"You'll be a *woman*," she called after me.

"I don't wanna be a woman," I said through tears, letting the door slam behind me.

DAWN MARANO

## Fallout

My father started digging a bomb shelter in our backyard
one Saturday when I was six. Our landscaping was rudimenta-
ry at best, and I see this working in my father's favor as he tried
to convince my mother that his undertaking wasn't impetuous
at all. *Hell, Glendora, there's hardly anything but dirt out there
anyway; might as well put the thing in now.* I doubt my mother
agreed to the plan—surrendered to it is probably closer—but
in whatever manner she acquiesced, I imagine my father feeling ennobled somehow as he took our safety and well-being
right into his own two, soon-to-be-calloused, hands.

On weeknights after work, he'd eat dinner then shovel
until it was too dark to see. It wasn't long before the kids next
door started asking questions, and I was told to say we were
building a swimming pool. We lived, like everyone else, in a
very modest suburban tract home, so this was an egregious lie,

in retrospect—but only a white lie, as my parents explained it. After the attack, they said, our subdivision would be overrun with marauding bands of irradiated neighbors who hadn't planned ahead for atomic fallout. We certainly wouldn't want them to know about our hideaway, would we?

My parents could be like this: doomsayers of the first order. But they were optimists, too—at least when it came to the consumption of durable goods. I suspect this dichotomy was not that unusual among postwar couples. Theirs was the first generation to deal with the concept of instantaneous mass annihilation; the first to be expected to hold images of mushroom clouds over Nippon in suspension with four-color ads for Frigidaires and Hoovers and Chevrolets. It's a lot to ask of a sane person.

I, of course, was too young to appreciate their predicament. All I knew was that we had a hole in our backyard big enough to inter a woolly mammoth or two, but nobody was ever going to swim in it. By the time I learned the truth of the matter, though, it was too late: Word about the pool had made the rounds, and my name had already shot to the top of the playmate popularity charts.

When my mother wasn't looking, I'd lie on the ground with my head over the lip of the pit, drawing in its mysterious, raw smell. The earth was dark and sodden; twisted roots appeared from unknown sources beyond our backyard walls. They reached into the great hole like fingers, seeking. I imagined my family together in the shelter with the roots folded around us, eating Campbell's soup, telling stories, waiting for the all-clear.

Then one day without any notice, my father filled the pit in again: broken cinder blocks, broken tools, broken lawn furniture, yard trimmings. Dirt, then sod.

After that, I think a part of me stopped counting on much of anything.

ROBERT SHAPARD

# Deep in the Art of Texas

I learned I didn't know who I was one summer evening when my father and mother and brother and my little cousin Camille and my grandparents, with whom we lived, were gathered around the table. It was only a passing remark yet it made me feel like the first fish that ever crawled onto land. In one exhilarating moment my fins turned into feet, and with my very first step I was lost.

There would be cross-breezes on evenings like these from the floor fan at one end of the room and the French doors open at the other, and June bugs on the screens, even if there was still sun caught in the curtains, which were sheer and light, behind my grandfather, they rose and fell hypnotically, furling and unfurling like the breathing of the long summer itself. (My grandfather was a New Englander, a civil engineer who came to Texas in 1905, a builder of streets and small bridges: very practical and taciturn.) My grandmother, at her end of the table, sat under the portrait of Judge Bonner, her father, who had come to Texas with his law degree from Tennessee after the Civil War, and who presided in his dark gold frame over all our meals. The famous Judge Bonner of the dark hair, the tanned and grooved and forbidding face, though at times there seemed a deep, benevolent humor in him; in his white shirtfront he seemed to rise out of the blackness of the background, judging and blessing us all. My grandmother, on the other hand, looked to me very much like George Washington with her hooded eyes, though with her own humor too: she had a shop on the third floor of the house, where in the mornings with torch and vise and acid vats she fashioned the leaves and blooms of metal flowers, or hammered out brass ashtrays with her mallets, then came down to lunch in her apron smelling faintly of propane gas and iron filings. Being young I had only a vague sense that she came from a line of Southern gentry to which I was at least partly heir. After all, she was the first woman in town to drive an automobile, and did as she pleased: she played poker and bet on the horses. In 1918, when she was a young woman, she had led our city's first Armistice Day parade dressed as Columbia and shocked everyone by showing her ankles.

"But wasn't Judge Bonner really a judge?" I heard my brother say. He was two years older than I and vastly more mature.

"Oh, his friends called him that," she said, salting her cantaloupe. "But he wasn't a judge, he was just a lawyer."

"He looks like a judge," my brother said.

My grandmother had hardly been paying attention to my brother. Now she blinked at him, then glanced a little over her shoulder toward Judge Bonner's portrait. "That's not him, you know. I don't know who that is. I bought him at an antique store sale."

My grandfather said, "Pass the fish."

Meantime the others were holding their own conversations, voices murmuring; someone thumped a waterglass down, and my cousin Camille kept kicking her feet under the table. For a while I could not take my eyes off the strange portrait; then could not take them off the summer evening blowing through.

JOHN EDWARDS

# Prison Man Considers Turkey

A first Thanksgiving in prison may be laden with maudlin sentimentality, and a last with hard-boiled familiarity, but in the middle are moments when clearly defined feelings fray and you can't be sure exactly who you are. During my first Thanksgiving season in prison, I was sitting alone in The Hole, and my last was mere weeks before I walked out of there, as they say, a free man. The second Thanksgiving the shock of being locked up was gone, as was the truculent refusal to enjoy anything pleasant a prison experience might offer. But gone also was the novelty, especially for my family, tired of long drives and disrupted holidays. This second Thanksgiving in federal prison was celebrated by someone called *Me*, but I didn't know quite who he was, and neither did anyone back home. He tutored crack dealers for their GED exams, taught Shakespeare on Thursday nights, but prison can absorb you, and he was becoming the kind of guy who would rather teach classes in prison than have visits from his family. Because family meant guilt and failed responsibility. By comparison, prison was freedom.

Chief Running Mouth, believing Thanksgiving to be a celebration of Native American genocide, had tried to get the black guys to join his boycott. Nobody was going to do *that*. Psycho, missing the point completely, had said, "What'd them Pilgrims ever do for me?" Snakebite added, "When the white man wants to feed me some good food for a change, you want me to do *what*?" Even Toilet Paper Man, ever fearful of cosmic rays emanating from the mess hall, was there along with Bed-Sore, Bird, Stoney, and all the rest of us, standing in line, hoping the best turkey wouldn't be gone by the time we got there.

I'd finally found a seat with my little tray of turkey when a guard came up and said, "Edwards, you got a visit." I eyed my food, then looked at the other guys at the table. "Here," I said, "any you guys want this?" I got up, leaving my decent federal Thanksgiving dinner to the vultures. Up in the visiting room, families were arriving. Some inmates would let their families wait while they ate, but for most of us, family came first, even if that meant missing a special meal. Still, it was hard not to be torn between family and your buddies, the ones with whom you ate and worked and watched movies and read books and wrote to lawyers, and counted the days. The ones who were cooking contraband right now.

I had been down long enough to know that while we waited for our official meal, an unofficial one was being prepared back in the cellblock living units. Former car thieves, now with contacts in the kitchen, would be sneaking trays of turkey and pumpkin pie out the back door. And the Italian guys could prepare a meal worth a prison sentence to eat. The marijuana growers were the next best. These were men in their

forties like me—exactly like me, middle-class ex-hippies bust-
ed with little gardens in our cellars. We like good food.

My four-year-old son ran up to me and gave me a big
hug. I looked at Mary. "Hi," I said tentatively, and got a dark
look in response. "What? What'd I do?" I asked. "What's the
matter with you?" she demanded. I thought about that one a
while. "Is something wrong?" I asked. "Just never mind," she
spat. Now, of course something was wrong. I was in prison for
growing marijuana and she was stuck alone with our child. As
guys were wolfing down my Thanksgiving dinner, I ate a
microwave mini-pizza from the vending machine and tried to
hear Mary, over the din of the visiting room, recite her stream
of complaints, which I could do nothing about. Prison visiting rooms are never comfortable, and on holidays they are
always crowded and hot and loud. This was our second
Thanksgiving here, and eighteen months of this was getting to
her. "You never give me what I need," she said. "I can't. I'm in
prison," I tried lamely. "We were waiting here for almost an
hour," she said. "Well, things were a little chaotic down in the
chow hall . . ." "Sometimes I think you'd rather be with your
friends than with us," she said. She wasn't far from wrong.

Each of us was torn, I between this hellish racket of the
visiting room and the camaraderie of the prison, and she
between this same hellish racket and the camaraderie that
would await her when she left me for the day: prison wives sitting around a Formica table in the motel restaurant, probably
ordering turkey dinner, bad-mouthing us and exchanging
nightmarish tales of handling the house and kids back home
alone with community and family disapproval looming over
their tired shoulders. We'd dragged them into this and now,
hundreds of miles from home, missing home-cooked dinners
at their own parents' houses, they were prison wives whose
children played together while we snuck food and cookery

behind the backs of the guards who themselves would rather have been home on Thanksgiving. It was our fault for putting everybody through this, and the guilt we felt was in part because, under these conditions, we knew we were beginning to prefer each other's company to that of our real families.

Visiting hours were over and I went back to my cell. A plate of turkey with all the clearly contraband goodies was waiting for me. Somebody, knowing I'd missed dinner, had cooked it up and made sure I got it. I have no idea who that might have been. Maybe Chief Running Mouth. Maybe Psycho.

ROBERT O'CONNOR

# The Left-Handed Sweeney and Vacation

### THE LEFT-HANDED SWEENEY

The first time Hector saw somebody killed in prison, he wrote in his journal, the hitter approached his victim from behind. It was a contract hit, and the hitter, a man already with a fifty-to-life sentence, began rhythmically stabbing his victim. The other men immediately put their backs to the wall to prevent anyone from taking advantage of the confusion by putting a knife where they'd always wanted. When he was done, and the man was dead, the hitter walked over to the guard who was calling for help and handed him the knife. What Hector remembered most, he wrote, was that everyone immediately pulled out cigarettes and began smoking, as if they had all just enjoyed great sex. I started reading Hector's journal at ten on a Saturday night. Six hours later, at four o'clock in the morning, I was still reading.

The journal was over two hundred pages long and recorded Hector's upbringing in a Catholic orphanage, and his life in karate as a teenager (it's likely that Hector and I had passed each other at New York City karate tournaments). He recorded how once working as a messenger, he had met Robert Redford; and how, while lifting weights, he had stopped to watch a monarch butterfly rest its wings on the chin-up bar. He didn't allow himself to watch television, he wrote, because he was afraid to become too involved in a show and fail to notice someone creeping up to stab him. He couldn't allow himself not to remember for a moment where he was. He was caught in a reality so fierce that it could not tolerate fantasy.

The journal was addressed to me, a long document expressly meant for my education. He had missed my name in the early going, but knew I was Irish and left-handed, and so the early entries were addressed to "the Left-Handed Sweeney." Despite being Hispanic, he was a member of the biker court due to his fighting prowess. This was unusual because the rest of the biker court was composed of white racists. He'd been brought in by a big, Irish biker, and he wrote that I reminded him of that man.

"Are you coming to bed?" Donna called from upstairs.

"In a while," I said.

## VACATION

I needed a week off from teaching at the prison and so I called in sick and volunteered to drive my mother-in-law down to New York City. I stayed with my parents and I read books that I'd been meaning to catch up on for the whole semester. On the drive back, I thought of the things I'd learned. It was the small things, in certain ways, that were the most terrible. For instance, there was a bank of phones at one edge of the Yard that the prisoners could use to make collect calls home. It turned out, according to Hector, all of the phones were owned.

"How do you own a phone?" I had asked.

"Easy, and not so easy," he said. "You go up and say, 'I own this phone.'"

"What if someone else owns that phone?" I asked.

"Someone else always owns it," Hector said. "That's the not-so-easy part."

VIVIAN GORNICK

# from "On the Street"

In the middle of the intersection at Thirty-fourth and Second two cars have nearly collided. Both are stopped at angles of craziness, doors flung open, each driver out of the car, screaming. Instantly, the crowd gathers. A cop walks over. Both drivers scream at him. "Man, you see what he did? You see what he *did?*" The cop places a hand on the arm of each man and says, "I'm now about to administer justice. You," he nods at one and points east, "get in your car. You," he nods at the other and points west, "get in your car. And both of you, get the fuck out of here." The crowd applauds.

On the corner of Twenty-third and Seventh a man with a navy blue wool cap jammed onto his head, shivering inside a fake leather jacket, stands selling an old *Daily News* for a quarter, on his face a sinister smile. The headline reads: SADDAM SHOT. The man calls out softly, "Read all about it. Read all about it. They're shooting at your friend and mine. Send him your love, send him a card, send him a bomb. Let him *know* how you feel." Closure at last on America in the Persian Gulf.

In front of the Coliseum a hawker stands selling some gadget that everyone is passing up. "One dolla, one dolla, only a dolla, folks," he drones. "Get it while you can. Just today, one dolla, one dolla." Only his mouth is moving, his face is silent, his eyes dead. A young woman passes in the crowd. She works in the neighborhood. The hawker knows her. "One dolla, only a dolla . . . Nice ta see ya, darlin, *nice* ta see ya, how are ya taday . . . A dolla, folks, only a dolla." It's shocking to hear his voice break the drone, quicken into life, resume the drone. Her cheeks color up. She doesn't mind. She nods in recognition. "Good," she says in a low tone and keeps moving. The expression on each face intensifies: on his pleasure, on hers relief. Clearly, it's a ritual. Thirty seconds a day these two rescue each other deep in the middle of the anonymous crowd.

The street keeps moving, and you've got to love the movement. You've got to find the composition of the rhythm, lift the story from the motion, understand and not regret that all is dependent on the swiftness with which we come into view and pass out again. The pleasure and the reassurance lie precisely in the speed with which connection is established and then let go of. No need to clutch. The connection is generic not specific. There's another piece of it coming right along behind this one.

On the Sixth Avenue bus I get up to give an old woman my seat. She's small and blond, wearing gold jewelry and a mink coat, her hands a pair of blotchy claws with long red fingernails. "You did a good thing, dear," she says to me and smiles coyly. "I'm ninety years old. I was ninety yesterday." I smile back at her. "You look fantastic," I say. "Not a day over seventy-five." Her eyes flash. "Don't get smart," she says curtly.

At a coffee counter two women sit talking at right angles to me. One is telling the other that an older woman she knows is sleeping with a much younger man. "All her friends keep saying to her, 'He wants your money.'" The woman at the counter nods her head like a rag doll and lets her face go daffy in imitation of the woman she's speaking of. "'Right,' she tells them. 'And he can *have* it. All of it.' Meanwhile, she looks great."

At Forty-eighth Street a couple catches my eye. His face is ghastly white, hers a mask of badly applied make-up. Their eyes are swollen slits inside pouches of alcoholic skin. Both are wearing tight cheap clothes, her hips bursting from the skirt, his belly pushing up beneath the T-shirt. She bends with a cigarette in her mouth to take a light from the match in his trembling hand. As I pass them she straightens up, exhales her first breath of smoke, and says, "You are starting with a negative attitude. That is not the way to do it."

The streets attest to the power of narrative drive: its infinite capacity for adaptation in the most inhospitable of times. Civilization is breaking up? The city is deranged? The century is surreal? Move faster. Find the story line more quickly.

I cut over to Broadway and continue on downtown. At Forty-second Street, crossing in a mob of people, the man in front of me—skinny, black, young—suddenly lies down spread-eagled in the middle of the street just as the cars are beginning to move. I turn wildly to the man walking beside me who, as it happens, is also skinny, young, black, and say to him, "Why is he *doing* this?" Without breaking his stride he shrugs at me, "I don't know, lady. Maybe he's depressed."

Each day when I leave the house I tell myself I'm going to

walk up the East Side of town because the East Side is calmer, cleaner, more spacious, easier to stride about in. Yet, I seem always to find myself on the crowded, filthy, volatile West Side. I don't exactly know why this happens, but more often than not, an afternoon on the West Side feels positively thematic. All that intelligence trapped inside all those smarts. It reminds me of why I walk. Why everyone walks.

CASTLE FREEMAN, JR.

## Stuck with Strangers

In going about my winter business in the country around Brattleboro, Vermont, I have gotten stuck in the snow and ice about fifteen times. That is not a lot for twenty-five winters' worth of driving in Vermont, much of it up and down a rugged elevation of some local fame called Newfane Hill, on whose side I live and whose ancient Algonquin name, I am told, means "Oil Trucks Put On Chains."

No, in these parts hitting the ditch an average of 0.6 times a year isn't bad at all. But more surprising to me than my relatively untroubled career in winter driving is the fact that of those fifteen or so mishaps only one has required a tow truck. One dark night I slid off Route 5 just north of Putney to such good purpose that I had to call the wrecker. But every other time I have come to grief, I have been put right without benefit of clergy, so to speak. Why? Because I have been helped by my fellow man. Friends, neighbors, perfect strangers, have stopped, lent a hand, and gone on their way.

Like every other longtime winter driver in Vermont, I have had many helpers—though to be honest, I should say more helpers than help. Through the long winters up here the icy mountain roads bring out some of the best, most altruistic instincts that people can have, but they bring them out by an elliptical route. For there is something in the sight of a car pathetically stranded on a snowy shoulder that inspires otherwise sensible men and women with the spirit of debate, the spirit of controversy. Getting helped out of a winter ditch by passing Good Samaritans, one finds oneself not only the grateful recipient of generous aid but also the object of a certain hill-country ritual of assistance.

A case in point:

On a bright January morning a couple of years ago, I was coming home up the hill, driving carelessly along trying to remember what, exactly, happened in the Defenestration of Prague, when suddenly I felt the hindquarters of my wagon begin to describe a counterclockwise arc—speedily, irresistibly, in a classic rear-end skid.

In this situation the advice of the experts is unanimous. You remain calm. You don't brake. You steer deftly in the direction of the skid, so that the momentum of the car can straighten it out. That is good advice—but I seldom follow it. I find that what works for me in a skid is to hit the brakes as hard as I can, shut my eyes, and repeat certain words at increasing volume until I land wherever I'm going to land.

So it happened that morning in January: the rear went east, the front went west, and the whole show, with me in it, wound up half on the road, half in the ditch, pointing back down the hill, and stuck, stuck, stuck.

At this point in any such debacle my procedure is always the same. I turn off the motor and get out of the car. I then walk around the car, examining it closely but dispassionately, as though it were no car of mine but one I have discovered inexplicably abandoned by persons unknown. Doing this introduces an element of disassociation into the episode which prepares me to receive help when it arrives.

Help arrived that morning in the form of two fellows in a truck. They stopped, got out, and joined me in surveying the problem. We agreed that the road was slick, the car was mine, the car was stuck. (Here and in the next several paragraphs I reduce a fairly prolonged and complex exchange to its essentials.)

"Not bad stuck," one of the men said to his partner. "He's headed downhill. He ought to start up, straighten his wheels, and just tickle the accelerator. Just ease it out."

"He doesn't want to ease it," the other said. "He wants to punch it. Get in. Start up. Straighten out. Then punch it. Punch it."

"He doesn't want to punch it," said the first. "He punches it, he'll dig in. He'll never get off. We'll have to pull him."

*Pull him*? I thought. *Yes.*

Another car came up the road and stopped. A young woman got out. She wore a red woolen hat with a pompon. She came over to the car, got down on her knees and looked underneath, brushed snow away from the ditched rear wheel, and looked some more. She stood.

"He ought to ease it," the first man said.

"He ought to punch it," the second man said.

"He's only spinning one tire," the young woman said. "He ought to throw the wheel hard left, put it in reverse, and back it up. That will make him roll off the patch he's spinning on. Then he gets into forward and drives right out. Easy."

"He doesn't want to reverse," the first man said. "He reverses, he'll get so far down in there he'll never get out. We'll have to pull him."

*Pull him?* I thought. *Why not?*

"Nobody's going to pull anybody," the young woman said. "Just do it," she said to me.

I did it. It didn't work. We had a storm of flying snow and dirt, and we had considerable screaming of tires, but I ended up a couple of feet farther down in the ditch than I had been, with my front end tilted now at a jaunty angle to the horizon. I got out of the car.

"It was worth a shot," the young woman said.

"I guess now we'll have to pull it?" I said.

"We can't pull it," the second man said. "We've got no chain."

"I've got a chain," the young woman said.

So the two fellows got her chain and hooked me up to their truck, and with them in the truck pulling, the young woman beside the car pushing, and me driving, we got me back in business easily enough. There followed the unhooking, the stowing of the chain, the thanks, the offer of payment, the offer's refusal, the return to the vehicles, the beep, the wave, the parting. Time elapsed since help arrived: twenty minutes. Time required for effective help to be applied: two minutes. Time required for advice: eighteen minutes. Exactly 90 percent of the transaction, therefore, was occupied not with practical assistance but with . . . what?

What was served? I'm not sure, but I suspect that these unhurried rural negotiations of suggestion and advice, assertion and doubt, amount to a kind of ceremony affirming a principle that many people—including, I'm afraid, me—prefer to neglect: Nobody does anything alone. Even those people who think they do—those people especially—need help, get help, take help gratefully, but never quite on their own terms. When your helpers arrive, they give what they have, in their own way, in their own time. Your part is to receive, to accept, and to learn, so that when you come to the same ceremony in the opposite role, you'll know what offering to bring. Someday the adviser will be you. What will you say?

I always tell them to punch it. "Punch it," I say. "Just punch it."

MICHAEL BLUMENTHAL

# Western Union

*Boise, Idaho, September 1996*

I've been out West before. Almost exactly twenty years ago—
in October of 1976 to be precise—at the invitation of the
poet Richard Hugo, I quit my job in Washington, D.C., sold
all the belongings that wouldn't fit into my used Toyota station wagon, broke up with my girlfriend, and moved to
Missoula, Montana.

It was a classic case, alas often repeated in my later life, of
the wrong act at the wrong time: after nearly a month in a
(pink, to my recollection) hovel called The Sweet Rest Motel
and a single night in a newly rented apartment, I woke,
stuffed my newly unpacked belongings back into my wagon,
fastened my seat belt, and, as they say in the West, "hightailed
it" back East just as fast as my panic-strickenly compressed gas

pedal could get me there. Within a month, I was working at Time-Life Books in Alexandria, Virginia, safely ensconced once again in a world of less sky and more concrete—a world where Europe, at least, was only an ocean away.

When people in those days asked me why I fled Montana in such a panic, my somewhat glib but not-untruthful response was a rather brief one: "Too American" I'd say, in only a slight variation of a phrase a friend of mine had once used to explain his flight from the suburbs: "Too many trees." The West—or what I saw and sensed of it at the time— indeed *was* too "American" for me, too filled, that is, with certain idiosyncrasies and intonations that perhaps only America, in all the world, properly owns. Nowhere else, for example, had I ever observed such a seeming disproportion of sky to earth, of nature to humanity, of wildlife to human life. Nowhere else had I ever walked into a bar where the main topic of conversation was how to find sufficient freezer space for your freshly slaughtered elk. Nowhere else had I ever encountered grandmothers and grandfathers who didn't speak with a German, Yiddish, or at least an Italian, accent. Nowhere else had I ever said "Thank you" to people and had them answer "You bet."

The West—particularly the "wild" West of places like Montana and Idaho—terrified me back in 1976 partly because, as I put it at the time, "It isn't on the way to any-where"—a kind second-generation euphemism for saying that it wasn't on the way to New York or Europe. America, in my immigrant-oriented eyes, was not so much America as an ocean-crossed extension of Europe, a place where you weren't "American," but merely a Greek, Italian, Pole, Hispanic, or Chinese living on borrowed turf. America was a place where you could take a walk in "nature"—i.e., an urban park—and still come out on the other side to find a bagel and a cappuccino. America was a place where a night crawler was an infant who had escaped from his crib.

Having spent the last four years in Central Europe, married to a French wife, and living recently as I have, in the Middle East, I've found that, for expatriates, America-bashing can become a kind of recreational activity ("re-creating," in the process, a sense of home), a way of both justifying your choices and reminding yourself, in a playful and not-too-disturbing way, of the country and culture that—despite anything and all you may do to have it otherwise—are yours. Part of the pride and pleasure of being an American, after all, is that there's so much to make fun of. (America, let's not forget, is the nation that has made comic self-mockery into an art form—and excessive love of country into a right-wing threat.)

"You loved them well and they remain," the poet Hugo wrote of the people in his small town, "still with nothing to do, no money and no will." And now, as I contemplate Hugo and Montana and Europe and Boise, it occurs to me that one of my own human failings may have been that—with all their human flaws, comedies, and foibles—I haven't loved my fellow Americans well enough. Twenty years, three continents, and two marriages later, I realize that what I may have been partly fleeing from when I took off in a purple haze from Missoula was a certain deeply rooted, though submerged, Americanness within myself.

Driving my rented car up Idaho Highway 21 out of Boise, past—where else could you find such a name?—Lucky Peak and toward the old Gold Rush town of Idaho City the other night, I found myself marveling at all that beautiful sky, the parched but massive ponderosa pines yearning for rain. Occasionally I stopped the car just to pause and inhale, and the air was so clean and still I could swear I heard the sound of some distant fly fisherman's fly touching down on a stream.

There wasn't a bagel or a cappuccino for miles, but I kept turning my head in all directions, hoping to spot an elk. If I stopped at the little twenty-four-hour grocery in the shack around the bend, I could be dead certain the person inside would speak English, the one language (all dilettanteries aside) I know well enough to truly love. "Home," wrote Robert Frost, "is the place where, when you want to go there, they have to take you in," and the chances that they will, seems to me, are a helluva lot better if you speak the same tongue.

Tonight in Boise, when I turn over early in my motel room to sleep, the frenzied crowd in the football stadium across the road, screaming their lungs out on behalf of the Boise State Broncos, will most likely keep me awake. There's sky all around me, and the closest thing to an accent I've heard thus far is the distinction between "upcountry"—the rural part of the state—and down. Thus far at least, though I've only been here a week, no one's asked me to stay. But, if they do, the odds are better than even money that, pausing for a moment to clear the other languages and international cobwebs from my too-long-exiled psyche, I'll turn for a moment, look up at the sky, and say, "You bet."

W. SCOTT OLSEN

# 107 Miles West of Fargo

There is a point in every trip when the car and the driver seem to settle into each other and, as a pair, settle into the road. Where the driving itself almost becomes transparent and you watch the landscape roll by at faster than a mile a minute.

There is a point in every trip when the driving becomes fun. Bright silver grain elevators, red barns, cattails in the marshes, redwing blackbirds, motorcycles and eighteen-wheel trucks all blend into a kind of moving diorama. From my point of view, I'm sitting still and the world is racing toward and then away from me, and I've got the Rolling Stones on the radio. Clear blue sky in front of me now. I've seen a dozen mountain ranges erupt and then dissipate in the clouds this morning. Lightning strikes, strong wind, mass annihilation of mayflies and an invitation to see an albino buffalo—and this trip is just beginning.

A little bit more than one hundred miles west of Fargo, and the landscape here rolls . . . what? To say the landscape rolls "gently" would imply too much action. Hay ricks and hay bales are stacked in some fields. The grains and the beans are still green. Harvest is a good way off. It's a midsummer on the prairie—full of promise and grace and a little bit of danger, too. And in front of me, still the gravity of those mountains. Those real mountains of stone and wood and ice and fluid need.

ANNICK SMITH

# Sink or Swim

Indian summer. Montana. Rivers. You get the picture. Sky-
blue waters gurgling with trout. Freckled cottonwood leaves
like a yellow flotilla. Kingfishers, rose hips, purple asters. For
me, eye-popping, soul-singing joy if that river is the Big
Blackfoot a few miles upstream from my house.

By late afternoon on such a day, the river calls to me—a
cathedral bell ringing, promising glory. The air is dry, hot, and
blue, and the topsoil along the bluff is fluffy as powder. As I
walk my dogs up the Blackfoot from Whitaker Bridge, I turn
my eyes from logged-off hills to the cleft green gorge where
the snake of bright waters unfurls.

I am walking under ponderosa pines, trailing my fingers
along reddish columns of picture-puzzle bark. The river is
splattered with yellow light, but the water runs green. The
Blackfoot is green as the scent of rain. Green as frogs and moss

and evergreen trees. I crush pine needles under my feet and their perfume mingles with the sharp odor of cottonwood sap and the trout-scent of water over stones. Larch shower needles of gold on my head.

These are the days of gold. I will dream of them during winter nights, the cold that may pounce, perhaps tomorrow, like a cougar from the selfsame forest.

Betty Boop, my big-eyed shepherd dog, and Little Red, part chow part golden retriever, race ahead on the trail of a squirrel. Summer tourists are gone, only one Jeep in the parking area. We head for a sandy beach that cuddles between arms of stone across from a great cracked tower of red rock. The rose-pink slabs rise like a Moorish castle above a tree-shaded pool.

I am sweating. The pool is inviting. I decide to take the last plunge of summer. But there on my beach, stretched out like a walrus on an aluminum lounge, is a huge naked man. He basks in rays of the sinking sun, and as my dogs sniff at his toes, he raises a listless hand, turns his head toward me, and waves.

I call my dogs and flee. Moving quickly through patches of poison ivy invasive as the nudist, I climb over a rocky headland, descend a fisherman's trail to a peninsula of silver-tossed willows. Betty and Red rush into the willows. There is a thrashing noise—a whitetail buck leaps from the brush and into the river. I watch him swim into the dappled current, head high, antlers gilded with sunlight. I am surprised to find myself winded. Then I realize I have not taken a deep breath from the moment I ran from the man. Naked. Buck. I laugh out loud at the pure surprising coincidence. An osprey dives from the sky.

My dogs bark. They are barking at a raft with four people that is bobbing toward us from a bend in the river. Fishing lines extend on each side, like glowing cobwebs.

"How's it going?" I shout.

"Pretty good," says one fellow.

"Gorgeous day," says a girl.

"Anyone upstream?" I ask.

"No. I think we're the last."

Good, I think, for I know there's another swimming hole just ahead. My bank lies in shadows, but on the opposite shore a huge rock catches the light, its striated face patterned chartreuse and orange with lichens. At its feet is a sunny, graveled beach. This will be my perfect, private island.

When the raft is out of sight, I strip off my shorts and T-shirt, leaving on my underpants and Tevas, and begin to ford the river. Ankle-deep, the water is not too cold, but as I wade to my thighs, it turns icy. I catch my breath. This is foolish. I should turn back, but I plunge in. I'm a strong swimmer. I have swum this river many days. But never in October. Never so alone. Never at sixty.

The current is stronger than it looks. I kick hard, turn my arms like windmills until I find myself in slower water. I crawl over slick stones—aqua, maroon, green—shivering toward shore. Although the sun still hits the great lichened rock, and the pebbled beach holds the day's heat, I am cold, exposed, a half-naked sixty-year-old crazy woman clutching her arms around her flabby stomach, her breasts. My dogs have followed. They spray me with water, wag their tails.

Going back I'll be smarter, I think. I will make my way upstream, then let the current carry me to the home shore, to my dry clothes, to safety and warmth. But I've forgotten that the river is low. Slime-covered stones extend far into shallow water before the current takes over. I'm crawling crabwise again. And when I reach the deep running water, it doesn't ride me homeward, but curves downriver to the pool where I started my upstream journey.

I'm winded before I get halfway across. I kick and stroke, kick and stroke. It seems I am going nowhere. My breath comes in gasps and the quickened beat of my heart pounds in my ears. Fear finds me now. Not fear of drowning, but fear that my strength will fail. I will be vulnerable as a leaf, at the mercy of the river. Pull harder, I instruct my arms. My arms obey.

Eventually I break through the current, goose-bumps all over. My long white hair plasters my face, water drips from my eyes like tears. I stumble toward my clothes, the dogs frolicking and nosing at my weak knees. Even dressed and standing in a patch of sun, I tremble with the knowledge of mortality. I am older and weaker than the person I imagined I was, cold to the bone. Get moving, I tell myself. Get your blood running.

I start walking upriver on a piney ledge toward Belmont Creek. My head aches. My feet drag. It will take an hour before I feel halfway normal.

A mile ahead I can see a jumble of sticks on a high snag—the bald eagle aerie on Goose Flats. A white-headed giant screams at me as he glides from his perch. I want to scream back, "Hey, you, I'm still alive, too!"

Here is what I learned my from Indian summer swim. Take no chances when you are dealing with a wild and precious river. Stay humble. The river is wider than it seems. Respect it. Death waits under slime-covered stones. Every living thing is mortal.

RICK BASS

## January 13

If you look out at the snow, and beyond it, trying to see
through it to the woods on the other side of the meadow, it
seems to come down fast, and your life, if you let it trick you
that way, seems to be just as hurried and frantic. But if you
remember to look at the snow like a child, or a Texan—gazing
up, trying to see where it originates—then the slowness into
which it falls, the paralysis of its journey, will drop you immediately into a lower, slower state, one where you're sure to live
twice as long, and see twice as many things, and be two times
as happy at the end. Snow's more wonderful than rain, than
anything.

Ravens call out as they fly through snow. They're surprised
by it, I think, it starts up so quickly—one second a gunmetal
sky, and the next all the snow emptying out of that gray color,
tumbling down. That touches new corners of my brain, things

never before seen or even imagined: the sight of a raven flying low through a heavy snowstorm, his coal-black, ragged shape winging through the white, the world trying to turn him upside down, trying to bury him, but his force, his speed, cutting through all that snow, all that white, and headed for the dark woods, for safety. For a few beautiful moments there's nothing in my mind but black, raven, and white. My mind never clearer, never emptier.

*

There's a strange thing about myself that I can't explain. When I walk in the woods, if it's not snowing, I feel like exactly what I am—a man, alone, walking in the woods. But if snow's falling—if it's snowing heavily, with that underwater hush everywhere, that cotton-stuffed-in-one's-ears silence of soft snow falling—I feel like an animal.

I've seen flakes as big as my fist, and monstrous, wet, stuck-together flakes as big as wadded-up sheets of newspaper, falling among the myriad other, smaller flakes—plummeting madly down, tumbling like planes crashing, but landing silently, or nearly so. I'm describing the onset of a blizzard, which is what it's beginning to do right outside the greenhouse window and over my home, my cabin, and Elizabeth one hundred yards down the trail.

I can still see the outline of the house, and in it all that is my life, the shape of it, through the heavy falling snow, but just barely.

Take nothing for granted.

ANN DAUM

# Calving Heifers in a March Blizzard

It's not usually so bad, I'm told. This spring blizzards have hit one after another, snow thawing into mucky puddles that freeze and thaw again, spread to brown lakes with the next storm. Usually my dad has two hired men who alternate night duty during calving seasons. This year our foreman, Jim, quit in February, leaving Mike, who is new to South Dakota and the ranching life; his wife, Diana; and myself, the rancher's daughter just out of college, to calve out the heifers. In a blizzard. I have learned about the signs of impending birth in heifers, the way a vulva slackens and gapes just before labor begins. I have learned to cut one black heifer from sixty and drive her into a barn she has no intention of entering. I have learned to slam the head gate shut on a wild heifer, grease my cupped hand and naked arm with Betadyne solution and lubricant before reaching in to check her cervix. But mostly I have learned about walking through endless pen slop and calves dying in the ice-skimmed snow between my hourly nighttime checks. This has nothing to do with the herd health classes I aced in college. This has everything to do with death and the hundreds of different ways a heart can freeze.

Nights run into days and again into nights, every hour the same, interrupted only by the wet of scorched coffee and birth water. I was supposed to be good at this. My father brags about my way with animals, my dedication to caring for sick foals, my soft heart toward any creature in pain. He hasn't seen me kick the poor dumb calves for dying. Throw their lifeless bodies into the truck a little harder than I have to. It's not that I don't care, but that I can't. It overwhelms.

And it never seems to end. Tonight is my turn to check the heifers, spare Mike the few hours he'll sleep until feeding begins just after dawn. The white-faced heifer staring at me from the labor pen of the tilting, red barn won't wait till dawn to calve. She's been laboring since ten o'clock, and it's two now. Time to give her a hand.

Outside I hear the wind pick up, dash pellets of ice against the ancient wall boards. I pray no other heifers will choose tonight to calve.

I chase the black white-face into the head gate as gently as I can, but I am not really gentle. She wouldn't move if I were. She struggles briefly, breath rushing through her open mouth, brown eyes rolled to white. She doesn't understand. I am washing down, scrubbing Betadyne in an orange smear nearly to my shoulder, when she moans with the next contraction. Her breath comes quickly, hanging in clouds above her nostrils. She moans again, back humping up this time to push.

I cup my hand, slide my fingers past her vulva, into the heat of her vagina. She clenches down on me in a hot fist, and I move no farther until she relaxes. I thrust farther inside, up past my elbow before the next contraction, then wait. Grope, wait, grope, wait. Everything feels the same in there: wet, tense, slick. I shift positions, tilt downward, toward the cervix, wonder if I'm helping things at all.

Then I feel the calf, catch the slick rod of a foreleg for an instant before it slips away. Wait, grope. Feel a hoof brush my wrist—a soft, porous hoof, pointing down, as it should.

The calf should be pointing out toward the vulva with his nose resting on his outstretched forelegs. This time something feels wrong. Both forelegs are there, pointing down, but no nose. The heifer shivers, mouth-open groan with the next push. I will my arm to relax, wait through the contraction, then slide my cupped hand up the slick little leg. No nose. Farther, and I find the nose pushed down, caught on the rim of the heifer's pelvis.

The calf moves a little with the next push, wet-mouth flutterings under my hand. This is one I can save, and I will. I push the stiff front legs back toward the cervix, back against nature, hoping to realign the calf's head between his front legs. The cow doesn't help, resists in the way that is known to her. She pushes harder. Pushes her calf's skull deep into her pelvis's bony pocket. There is no way out for the calf in this position.

I push harder too, waiting for another break between contractions to wrestle the heavy calf farther back into his mother's womb. Finally feel the snot-slick ball of forehead tucked deep between his knees. I slide my palm down the curve of his nose, insert two fingers into his spongy mouth. He holds my fingers with his unborn tongue, tasting blood and air and life. The next contraction nearly breaks my arm and I groan with the cow. Nothing is so lonely and yet so entwined with another life as assisting a birth. I am up to my armpits in the creation of life. I feel three heartbeats pulse as one.

"Hold on, mother," I say to the heifer. "We're almost there." She seems to hear me, breathes out in short little gasps, prepares to push again.

The calf still clamps my fingers in his mouth, tight between his hungry pad of gums. I push backwards again on his front legs, hard this time, then pull his head up by the gums and lay it between his knees. Yes! He is outside his mother in under a minute, bleeding gently from the torn umbilical, sneezing straw tickles from his wide, wet nostrils. The heifer rests, uncaring, as I string the black bull calf upside down from one hind foot to weigh him. He protests, bawling through his birth-wet mouth. His mother hears this finally and stumbles up to take a look. Wonder, snuffling mother love.

I watch for a while, marvel with his mother at curious brown eyes fringed with thick black lashes, at tottering legs unfolded and propped up, one in each corner. The heifer noses her baby, then jumps when he falls back into the straw. I laugh, rinse my puckered arms in rust-flecked well water, then shrug back into my coat. The calf is on his feet again, and this time open mouth and curling baby tongue connect with teat and all is well. I'll check them again at three-thirty, but right now I want to go back to sleep. Dream for an hour of life, rather than death.

Outside, wind dries the sweat from my face, presses sleet through my woolen scarf. I pull open the barnyard gate, whump it closed, and begin a boot-clumping run for the house. The cold whistles through and around me, scorching my cheeks and the back of my throat. I laugh into the wind, and I am not numb.

GUY LEBEDA

# Man of Letters

I met Doug on the wrestling mat when we were in the seventh grade. By the time we reached high school we were good friends and by college we were best friends. It was after our college years, when Doug took a job teaching high school history in a town called Rawlins, Wyoming, that our correspondence began.

We started by exchanging a letter a week and discovered immediately that letter writing suited us both right down to the ground. After a month or so, we dropped the habit of calling each other because a phone call so often spoiled a good letter in the making. We only used the telephone in emergencies or when good news became urgent.

These letters from Doug—the ones I remembered to save—are all shapes and sizes, written on computer printout paper, spiral notebook pages (their ragged edges catching on

the other letters), cocktail napkins . . . one is even on sta-
tionery. We wrote about everything. When his young dog was
accidentally killed as a stray by the pound, Doug wrote a letter
filled with grief and outrage. When a favorite student quit
high school to work as a roughneck in the oil fields, Doug
wrote another long letter mourning that boy's lost future.
When Doug's son, Garrett, was born, he started a letter to me
in the hospital cafeteria that same night.

Sometimes a letter could be triggered by a stray thought
or an impression. "Dear Guy," one letter begins, "I just drove
through a magnificent thunderstorm, and that seems like reason enough to write to you now."

In February of 1984, Doug called me at my work. He was
in Denver, he said. At St. Joseph's Hospital, he said. "A galloping nosebleed that would not be stemmed. These doctors
want to run some tests." It was non-Hodgkins lymphoma.
The medics were quite optimistic, even chipper. But the treatments were long and hard. So, while he took steroids and was
irradiated within an inch of his life, I wrote him letters about
the raw, wet spring creeping slowly onto the Wyoming plains.

All his hair fell out. He underlined the word "all." He
gained twenty-five pounds from taking the steroids. He
became fish-belly pale, almost transparent, and had shadows
under his eyes the color of bruises. "You look like Uncle Fester
from the Addams family," I told him in a letter after a visit.

The treatments did their work. Doug went into something called remission, "a kind of stay of execution," Doug
called it. The next fall he was back teaching, and even coached
the junior varsity wrestling team. We went back to our habit
of writing once a week, and back to the usual topics of family,
careers, thunderstorms. I moved my family to Florida, but we
hardly missed a beat in our conversation.

In the spring of 1987 he wrote that he wanted to come for

a visit. He said I sounded like a propagandist for the Florida Tourism Board, and he wanted to see the place for himself. When school ended in May, he and Garrett came to Tallahassee. We visited Marineland, toured St. Augustine, and fished for blue crabs in the Gulf of Mexico. We talked for hours on end, but he was strangely silent at odd times, and one night as we drove home late from the beach, in the flash of passing headlights, I noticed tears in Doug's eyes as he held his sleeping boy on his lap.

Shortly before the end of their visit, Doug and I went for a walk through my suburban neighborhood. As we strolled through the fragrant darkness, he was suddenly swarmed by fireflies. He was completely enveloped in a gentle cloud of flickering lights. We stood looking at each other, while the insects hovered around him. After what seemed like a long time, the swarm floated away, and I shivered strangely in the hot night air.

Within a month, Doug was back in the hospital, taking more chemotherapy and losing ground to his disease. The medics tried more aggressive treatments, but by Thanksgiving they were admitting defeat. The only thing left was a bone marrow transplant. Doug's younger sister was found to be a suitable donor, and they all flew out to California for the surgery. I was writing about three letters per week. They were about anything and everything. He craved talk about the world outside the antiseptic walls.

He wrote whenever he could, but the letters were often in his wife Sylvia's handwriting. More and more they were also in her voice, her expressions. I tried hard to keep the pace of three per week. "They mean so much to him now," Sylvia wrote.

She called on a sunny December morning. "He's gone," she said. "He didn't regain consciousness after surgery." She sounded calm and brave. She asked me to give a eulogy. "Of course," I said. "I'm honored."

We drove straight through from Tallahassee to Laramie, dodging blizzards and black ice. We arrived late on the night before the funeral. Next morning I sat at my in-laws' kitchen table, trying to think of something to say about Doug. Nothing came to mind: not a word, not a picture. I thought of facing a church full of mourners and my mind was as blank as the page in front of me. I couldn't do it. I would have to beg off from this sad duty. The moment I made this decision, my hand grabbed the pen.

"Dear Doug," I wrote, "I know it's not my turn to write, but I just drove through a blizzard in Raton Pass, and that seems reason enough to write to you now."

YUSEF KOMUNYAKAA

# The Deck

I have almost nailed my left thumb to the 2 x 4 brace that holds the deck together. This Saturday morning in June, I have sawed 2 x 6s, T-squared and leveled everything with three bubbles sealed in green glass, and now the sweat on my tongue tastes like what I am. I know I'm alone, using leverage to swing the long boards into place, but at times it seems as if there are two of us working side by side like old lovers guessing each other's moves.

This hammer is the only thing I own of yours, and it makes me feel I have carpentered for years. Even the crooked nails are going in straight. The handsaw glides through grease. The toenailed stubs hold. The deck has risen up around me, and now it's strong enough to support my weight, to not sway

with this old, silly, wrong-footed dance I'm about to throw
my whole body into.

Plumbed from sky to ground, this morning's work can take
nearly anything! With so much uproar and punishment, foot-
work and euphoria, I'm almost happy this Saturday.

I walk back inside and here you are. Plain and simple as the
sunlight on the tools outside. Daddy, if you'd come back a
week ago, or day before yesterday, I would have been ready to
sit down and have a long talk with you. There were things I
wanted to say. So many questions I wanted to ask, but now
they've been answered with as much salt and truth as we can
expect from the living.

M ARY  C LEARMAN  B LEW

# from "Dirt Roads"

On a warm Friday morning in September of 1983, my father climbed in his old red truck and drove away from the ranch in the foothills of Montana's Snowies. He was on his way to Roundup to haul home a load of coal, seventy miles there and seventy back. It was a trip he had made two or three times a year for thirty years. The weather had been dry and cloudless with all the endless false promises of fall in Montana, and he would have driven out of the shade of pines with the sun at his back, soon out of sight of the sandstone ranch house, the sawed-board corrals, and the warm sorrel back of his favorite mare, Kallie, grazing in the home pasture.

Seven miles down from the foothills, in Lewistown, he filled up at a self-service gas station on Main Street, and the manager—one of the last people who talked to him—said later that when he came in to pay her, he told her where he was going, and that he seemed happy to be on his way. Then he drove out of town, southeast.

The mine where he had bought his coal for so long is a few miles north of Roundup. Even in his slow old truck, he should have reached it in a couple of hours. But at dawn on Saturday my sister Jackie called me from Havre to say that he never had stopped at the mine, never came home. Instead— from what we later were able to reconstruct—he drove past the side road and continued on Montana 87 into Roundup itself. Then he turned off the main street of Roundup onto Montana 12 to Forsyth and a part of the state he had never seen before. There is no logical accounting for his direction. The last time I was in Roundup, I circled back and drove through town a second time, showing myself how unlikely it would be for anyone to turn off the main street by accident or through confusion onto the Forsyth highway.

My sister and I knew nothing of this until much later. Although neither of us spoke it aloud, we both believed he had fallen asleep at the wheel and had rolled off the highway into some nameless, brush-choked coulee. My sister took my mother in with her and the children, while her husband spent the rest of the night driving and redriving the highway between Lewistown and Roundup.

But in fact, my father had driven to Forsyth and spent the night there in a motel. The next morning, Saturday, he paid his bill with a personal check and drove on east, away from home, angling south into some of the most sparsely settled territory in the world. And by midafternoon a report came to my sister—who had spent a sleepless night and a day making futile telephone calls to me, to the sheriff, to Search and Rescue, to me again—from the sheriff of Custer County, three hundred miles away, that he had been sighted at a remote ranch some thirty miles southeast of Miles City.

He had driven up to the ranch gate and stopped. I imagine him rolling down the window and scanning the miles of sagebrush and mirages between him and the horizon with the long-sighted blue eyes of the cattleman, searching for signs of life, of movement.

The rancher, working around the place, noticed the strange truck and felt uneasy about it—he had been robbed a few months earlier—so he went out to see what was up.

My father introduced himself by name. There followed a silence broken only, as I imagine it, by the wind rippling the sere September grass, a silence incomprehensible, perhaps, to anyone who has not lived in the western plains states. The two men would have waited, unhurried, the one in the cab of his dusty outfit, leaning his elbow out the window, the other with his arm on the gatepost, both of them dressed in their ordinary working clothes of scuffed boots and dirty Stetsons, Levi's, and ragged scarves, both of them with eyes not on each other but on the grass, the sky, the buildup of clouds and the approach of the first winter storm.

"If you'd met him," my cousin Willie told me later, "you'd have known he was another old Montana rancher like your dad, and the last thing he would have done was ask another man his business."

But the other rancher did begin to realize that, while he was in no risk of being robbed, he could not quite account for what he was seeing. "Anything wrong?" he asked, finally.

"No," said my father. He put his truck in gear and drove away, east and out of sight on a dirt road that would have led, eventually, to the South Dakota line. The other rancher, after mulling over the whole uneasy episode for several hours, decided to report it to the Custer County sheriff.

Jackie and I, going over and over this story, were relieved of our secret nightmares of the wrecked truck, the brushy gully, but we were perplexed by the direction and the purpose of our father's odyssey. What did he think he was doing? And why? *South Dakota?* A man who had preferred, all his life, to remain within twenty miles of his birthplace? What was he doing?

Still, we called our sister Betty in California to tell her that surely in a few hours we would have better news. Our father had been sighted alive and rational; surely he would be found soon, and we would know why.

But Saturday night fell, and with Sunday morning came the storm into eastern Montana. Rain and overcast and no further word.

"What was he wearing?" I asked Jackie over the phone.

"Long-handled underwear. And a wool shirt," she added.

We were silent, drawing what comfort we could from the thought of his wool shirt.

"Do you want me to drive down?" It was our unacknowledged code question.

"No. Not yet."

Every dragging hour meant less chance, and yet Search and Rescue, we learned, would not set out until a vehicle had been located. The heavy overcast in eastern Montana was keeping search planes on the ground. No word. No word.

What sustained us was not officialdom but the extended family network that had spread over the state. Cousins we had never met called their cousins in eastern Montana, and their children and relatives turned out, combing country roads and pastures on dirt bikes and on foot. Finally, on Monday afternoon, the persistent overcast began to lift, until cousin Willie, the pilot, could get his plane off the ground in Lewistown and head for Miles City. He spotted the red truck, and my father's body, within the hour.

"Do you want me to drive down?"

"Yes."

After the funeral, Willie drew my sisters and me aside to tell us what he had seen. Apparently my father had driven a few miles along the dirt road beyond the gate where he had talked to the other rancher, and he had parked the truck under a low hill overlooking a reservoir. In the distance he would have seen sage and sky, the blue outline of a butte, and the long blue bend of the Powder River. It looked a lot, Willie said, like the bend of the Judith River around the old homestead where my father was born and had spent his young manhood. It appeared as though he had gotten out of the truck and walked a few yards down the hill toward the reservoir, where a few cattle were grazing. Then he lay down on the slope and put his head on his arm as though to sleep.

My initial reaction to my father's death was less grief than a mixture of awe and rage. The awe was that he had achieved what Richard Hugo writes about in one of his last poems, "Death in the Aquarium."

> Where should we die given
> a choice? In a hothouse? Along a remote
> seldom traveled dirt road? Isn't some part
> of that unidentified man in us all
> and wants to die where we started?

My rage was at my father's acquiescence to that romantic and despairing mythology which has racked and scarred the lives of so many men and women in the West. The design by which he perceived his life can be traced clearly in his favorite books. During his last years he read and reread those old favorites—Louis L'Amour, Zane Grey, A. B. Guthrie—until it came to seem to me that his life was being transposed seamlessly into a chapter of the quiet rigor of *Arfive* or *The Last Valley*. I often wondered whether his fiction offered a

pattern for his sense of himself, or a mirror. But so strongly
did he believe in a mythic Montana of the past, of inarticu-
late strength and honor and courage irrevocably lost, that I
cannot escape the conviction that a conscious choice shaped
the way he died.

R. H. HERZOG

# Twigs

I am snowshoeing in my father's woods while the others are cleaning up and getting on with the rest of the day-after-breakfast. No one thought my father, at age ninety-one, should accompany me; not even my father thought so.

Last summer we walked in the woods, he behind me for perhaps the first time in our lives, he breaking off the ends of branches, twigs. When I asked him why, he explained, smiling, embarrassed, that last week he had lost his way, couldn't find the path back, lost in the woods he first encountered in 1914 and walked in for most of the rest of his life.

I kidded him. "Why break off the twigs when, even if you find them, you won't remember why?"

Now, in the snow, there is no sound of his laughter. No sound at all when I'm still, no bluejay or squirrels or chipmunks. Only a distant crow, and the creak of the leather binding on the ash frame of the snowshoes when I resume my walk under snow-laden hemlocks. I notice the trees fallen over the trails my father always kept clear.

I think of somehow framing in my memory forever the beauty of all these evergreens bearing the snow on sagging shoulders. And the silver beech trees somehow holding to their pale-yellow paper-leaves when all other deciduous trees, even the oaks, are barren, save for the snow.

But I know I can never remember all this, cannot even at this moment see it all. Couldn't capture it with all the cameras invented, wide-angled lenses, camcorders. It is too much for anything born or invented.

I remember Zen, that I haven't meditated since we've come down for the Christmas visit, too awkward with all of the people about. Now I am alone and unable to see all that is around me.

I am standing among fallen beeches sprawled across rocks three or four feet high, heightened by the drifted snow. Straight in my path, causing me to pause, consider, a fifteen-foot hemlock. Silver slivers of snow slant through the clearing.

I focus on one hemlock twig, green needles half-penetrating the snow puff upon it. I breathe from my *hara*, exhaling my breath into the universe. I will know forever this twig. Of all the twigs in the forest, this has been seen.

The next morning I follow the tracks of my snowshoes. I creak on snowshoes through trees creaking in the regenerating wind, to the spot where I yesterday meditated on the hemlock twig. I know the spot for the snow is more compacted here. I move my shoes into yesterday's tracks and stare intently at the hemlock starkly green against the snow. The twig is not there.

BRENDA MILLER

# Artifacts

### ANGEL

Once, in Sonoma, I bought an angel suspended from a twig. Her head is a polished knob of wood the size of my thumb; her hair, a mass of curly white thread. Her body's a thin shave of wood the color of cream. She's surrounded by strings of gold stars, and in her arms more stars cluster, overflowing. I know this mobile's supposed to dangle over a child's crib, dispensing blessing, but I have no child. So it hovers in a corner of my bedroom, and I watch from my bed, late at night: the twisting stars, the oblivious angel.

I saw it in a toy store on Main Street, while walking with my godson Sean. We glanced sidelong at each other as we loitered until his father got off work. I wanted to hold his hand, but I didn't dare; he was eight years old, a man already, and as we browsed the store windows we grunted to each other in low, indecipherable voices. At the toy store Sean wanted to buy a present for his mother and, with relief, we went our separate ways. He looked at clay earrings and stuffed monkeys; I touched this angel with my fingertips, tracing the Magic Marker crescents of her eyes, the red dot of her mouth.

As the angel drifted in her limited circle, I thought about Sean's birth, in the round shack at Orr Hot Springs, his head crowning, the turned shoulders, the body rollicking onto the bloody sheet. I remembered holding him twenty minutes later, in the rocking chair by the window as the morning ascended outside the glass. He still smelled of the womb; he tapped his white, wrinkled fingers against his lower lip, like an old man reminiscing. His gaze seemed all peripheral, and as I stared at him I said words I've never said before or since.

Of course Sean's forgotten, but I know he remembers *something*. As a toddler he sometimes looked at me oddly and babbled about our "special place," asked me to take him there. I walked with him down to the bend in the river and threw stones into the water, kneeling with him in the wild grass.

I went back to the store later, alone, and bought the angel for five dollars. The saleslady asked if it were a present, if I would like it wrapped, and I said, oh yes, that would be nice. It attracts whatever light seeps into the bedroom, fragments light into octagonal bits of stars. The angel's eyes are always closed, her mouth forever open in a red "Oh" which I take to mean singing, but which could just as easily be surprise, admonition, a yawn.

## SHELL

A fragment of a snail shell, bleached white, the whorl in the middle a bluish brown that sprouts to a point like a diminutive nipple. I found it on Whidbey Island, on a cold February afternoon. I had my own cottage in the woods, and in the mornings I sat in the window seat and wrote letters to my friends about the progress of the forced hyacinth I had brought with me from Seattle: "Its folded body still so green . . . I feel like that bulb, just now opening, but perhaps before my time. . . ." I wrote to them about growing older, about my fear of being alone and childless as I aged.

I usually grew discouraged in the afternoons, when the light no longer looked so promising through the pines, and so I got on my bicycle and pedaled for seven or eight miles along the coastal road, churning up hills, past gardens with stuffed owls to keep away the starlings. Or sometimes I just pedaled a mile to Useless Bay, and walked there at low tide, watching the sanderlings scuttle out of my path.

The shell was buried in the sand, the same color as the sand, camouflaged. I unearthed it and put it on my windowsill, gazed at it till it hypnotized me. Sometimes it became an eye, staring back, asking me to go deeper, to follow that spiral path into the center. Sometimes it disappeared in the dome light of afternoon. Other shells lay scattered on the path outside my cottage door, disintegrating under my feet, scattering into mosaic. Intertwined with the broken bodies lay feathers from the legs of an owl, dried needles of fir, cedar cones, footprints of invisible deer.


## AN UNEARTHED CRYSTAL

In the garden of my house at Orr Hot Springs I dug up a round crystal while trying to dig under the compost. I struck it with the edge of my spade, picked it out of the dirt, brought it inside and washed it at the kitchen sink. I strung it with a piece of mint-green dental floss, hung it in the loft window. Seth came upstairs as I touched it, as it threw truncated rainbows across the sun-yellow ceiling. Look what I found, I said and he said Lovely, then kissed me behind the ears, down my neck to the place where the change begins, where the head becomes the body, and the body knows nothing of its own bounds. I lay back with him—I was still young, he was not, our love already disintegrating, turning to shards dangerous and elusive as glass. But he traced the scar below my belly button, his fingers inexplicably kind, forgiving. My crystal knocked against the window, twisted on its string, transformed whatever light happened to fall upon our skin.

## DEAD PEOPLE'S THINGS

My grandfather's silverware, adorned with roses, the initial "M" engraved in the handle of each utensil. My grandmother's linen handkerchiefs, monogrammed with the same "M," yellowed around the edges. Books from people I never knew, bought at bookstores with dusty shelves and dim lights, the inscriptions on the flyleaves sheared of any luster, sad now in the wrong hands. A wedding photograph of my grandmother and grandfather, my grandmother's hands covered in flowers, her eyes focused on a place that does not include me.

## EMPTY VESSELS

A glazed bowl from Mendocino, swirled in pastels of blue and pink; a green-striped pitcher from Portugal; a blue vase from Italy, the glass pale and veined with ivy; a reed and willow basket from Montana, braids of acorns dangling from the handle. I like the fact of their emptiness; not only the clean lines of the vessels themselves, sharp against their backdrops, but the empty space they shape and contain. I'm tempted to leave these vessels empty forever, to forgo the cut flowers, the coins, the fruit.

My Zen teacher told me "emptiness is form and form is emptiness," a phrase I repeated but never understood until now, as I lie on my rug in my new apartment and gaze at these forms which keep changing under my eye. One moment they are clearly containers; the next moment they are contained by what surrounds them. I've often thought of my body as empty, in a negative sense: infertile, gaping, hollow. I've envisioned the cup of my barren pelvis as a void: dark and unfathomable, a body perverted by the fact of its emptiness.

Two people I know died in their sleep this week. As I think about them, their empty bodies float in my mind— sometimes light, unfettered; sometimes heavy and inert as lead. Both died of heart failure: a forty-nine-year-old woman and a nineteen-year-old girl. And, as I surround myself with empty vessels, I become aware of my own heartbeat, the shallow labor of my lungs against my ribs. *Form is emptiness, emptiness form*, I repeat to myself, and with that hymn my body starts to hum, to be filled.

BRIAN DOYLE

## Two Hearts

Some months ago my wife delivered twin sons one minute
apart. The older is Joseph and the younger is Liam. Joseph is
dark and Liam is light. Joseph is healthy and Liam is not.
Joseph has a whole heart and Liam has half. This means that
Liam will have two major surgeries before he is three years old.
The first surgery—during which a doctor will slice open my
son's chest with a razor, saw his breastbone in half, and reconstruct the flawed plumbing of his heart—is imminent.

I have read many pamphlets about Liam's problem. I have
watched many doctors' hands drawing red and blue lines on
pieces of white paper. They are trying to show me why Liam's
heart doesn't work properly. Blue lines are for blood that needs
oxygen. Red lines are for blood that needs to be pumped out
of the heart. I watch the markers in the doctors' hands. Here
comes red, there goes blue. The heart is a railroad station

where the trains are switched to different tracks. A normal heart switches trains flawlessly two billion times in a life; in an abnormal heart, like Liam's, the trains crash and the station crumbles to dust.

There are many nights just now when I tuck Liam and his wheezing train station under my heart in the blue hours of the night and think about his Maker. I would kill the God who sentenced him to such awful pain, I would stab Him in the heart like He stabbed my son, I would shove my fury in His face like a fist, but I know in my own broken heart that this same God made my magic boys, shaped their apple faces and coyote eyes, put joy in the eager suck of their mouths. So it is that my hands are not clenched in anger but clasped in confused and merry and bitter prayer.

I talk to God more than I admit. Why did you break my boy? I ask. I gave you that boy, He says, and his lean brown brother, and the elfin daughter you love so. But you wrote death on his heart, I say. I write death on all hearts, He says, just as I write life. This is where our conversation always ends, and I am left holding the extraordinary awful perfect prayer of my second son, who snores like a seal, who might die tomorrow, who did not die today.

STUART DYBEK

# Thread

The year after I made my First Holy Communion, I joined the Knights of Christ. So did most of the boys in my fourth grade class. We'd assemble before Mass on Sunday mornings in the sunless, concrete courtyard between the convent and the side entrance to the sacristy. The nuns' courtyard was private, off limits, and being allowed to assemble there was a measure of the esteem in which the Knights were held.

Our uniforms consisted of the navy blue suits we'd been required to wear for our First Holy Communion, although several of the boys had already outgrown them over the summer. In our lapels we wore tiny bronze pins of a miniature chalice engraved with a cross, and across our suitcoats we fit the broad, satin sashes that Sister Mary Barbara, who coached the Knights, would distribute. At our first meeting Sister Mary Barbara instructed us that the responsibility of the

252 ■ IN BRIEF

Knights was to set an example of Christian gentlemanliness. If ever called upon to do so, each Knight should be ready to make the ultimate sacrifice for his faith. She told us that she had chosen her name in honor of St. Barbara, a martyr whose father shut her up in a tower and, when she still refused to deny her Christian faith, killed her. I'd looked up the story of St. Barbara in *The Lives of the Saints*. After her father had killed her—it didn't say how—he'd been struck by lightning and so St. Barbara had become the patron of fireworks and artillery, and the protectress against sudden death.

Our sashes came in varying shades of gold, some worn to a darker luster and a bit threadbare at the edges, and others crisp and shining like newly minted coins. We wore them diagonally in the swashbuckling style of the Three Musketeers. It felt as if they should have supported the weight of silver swords ready at our sides.

Once outfitted, we marched out of the courtyard into the sunlight, around St. Roman Church, and through its open massive doors, pausing to dip our fingers in the marble font of holy water and cross ourselves as if saluting Our Lord—the bloodied, life-sized Christ crowned with thorns, in the vestibule. Then, we continued down the center aisle to the front pews that were reserved for the Knights.

In the ranking order of the Mass we weren't quite as elite as the altar boys, who got to dress in actual vestments like the priest, but being a Knight seemed an essential step up the staircase of sanctity. Next would be torchbearer, then altar boy, and beyond that, if one had a vocation, subdeacon, deacon, priest.

Though I couldn't have articulated it, I already understood that nothing was more fundamental to religion than hierarchies. I was sort of a child prodigy when it came to religion in the way that some kids had a gift for math or spelling.

Not only did I always know the answer in catechism class, I could anticipate the question. I could quote scripture and recite most any Bible story upon command. Although I couldn't find my way out of our parish, the map of the spiritual world was inscribed on my consciousness. From among the multitude of saints, I could list the various patrons—not just the easy ones like St. Nicholas, Patron of Children, or St. Jude, Patron of Hopeless Cases—but those that most people didn't even know existed: St. Brendan the Navigator, Patron of Sailors and Whales; St. Stanislaus Kostka, Patron of Broken Bones; St. Anthony of Padua, whose name, Anthony, I would take later when I was confirmed, Patron of the Poor; St. Bonaventure of Potenza, Patron of Bowel Disorders; St. Fiacre, an Irish hermit, Patron of Cab Drivers; St. Alban, Patron of Torture Victims; St. Dismas, the Good Thief who hung beside Christ, Patron of Death Row Inmates; St. Mary Magdalen, Patron of Perfume.

I could describe their powers with the same accuracy that kids described the powers of Super-Heroes—Batman and Robin, Green Lantern, the Flash—but I knew the difference between saints and comic-book heroes: the saints were real.

I didn't doubt either their existence or their ability to intercede on behalf of the faithful with God. In the dimension of the spiritual world there was the miraculous and the mysterious, but never the impossible. At each Mass, we would witness the miraculous in the transubstantiation of bread and wine into the body and blood of Christ. And when I encountered mysteries such as the mystery of the Trinity or the mystery of the Holy Ghost, I believed. Mystery made perfect sense to me.

My holy medal turning green around my neck, I practiced small rituals: wore a thumbed cross of ashes on my forehead on Ash Wednesday as a reminder of mortality, wore a scapular wool side against the skin of my chest as a reminder of suffering, suffering that I could offer up as I offered up the endless ejaculations I kept careful count of for the Poor Souls in Purgatory.

That was an era for ceremony, a time before what my pious aunt Zosha came to derisively refer to as Kumba-ya Catholicism, when the Mass was still in Latin, and, on Good Fridays, weeping old women in babushkas would walk on their knees up the cold marble aisle to kiss the relic, a glass-encased sliver of the True Cross, that the priest presented at the altar rail. After each kiss, he would wipe the glass with a special silk kerchief for sanitary purposes.

In those days, to eat meat on Friday, the day of Christ's Crucifixion, was a mortal sin that could send a soul to Hell. Before receiving Communion, one was required to fast from the night before. To receive Communion without fasting was a mortal sin, and there could be no greater blasphemy than to take the body and blood of Christ into one's mouth with mortal sin on the soul. Sometimes at Sunday Mass, women, weak from fasting, would faint.

Once Mass began, the Knights would rise in unison and stand and kneel to the ebb and flow of the ceremony with a fierce attention that should have been accompanied by the rattling of our sabers and spurs against the marble. Our boyish, still unbroken voices were raised in prayer and hymn. At Communion time, it was the privilege of the Knights to be the first to file from the pews, leading the rest of the congregation to the Communion rail. There we would kneel in a long row while the priest, often Father Pedro, the first Mexican priest at our parish, who'd served in the Marine Corps as a chaplain and lost an eye to shrapnel while administering the last rites to dying soldiers in Sicily, distributed the Eucharist to us as if reviewing the troops. Usually, Father Pedro wore a brown glass eye, but he'd been breaking glass eyes lately—the rumor was he'd been going out drinking with Father Bogulaw—and when he'd break one he'd wear a pair of sunglasses with the lens over the good eye popped out.

Sometimes, approaching the Communion rail, I'd be struck by the sight of my fellow Knights, already kneeling, by their frayed cuffs and the various shades of socks and worn soles. It never failed to move me to see my classmates from the perspective of their shoes.

One Sunday, sitting in the pew, watching flashes of spring lightning illuminate the robes of the angels on the stained glass windows, my mind began to drift. I studied my gold sash upon which the tarnishing imprint of raindrops had dried into vague patterns—it had begun to rain just as we marched in off the street. There was a frayed edge to my sash and I wrapped a loose thread around my finger and gently tugged. The fabric bunched and the thread continued to unwind until it seemed the entire sash might unravel. I pinched the thread and broke it off, then wound it back around my finger tightly enough to cut off my circulation. When my fingertip turned white, I unwound the thread from my finger and weighed it on my open palm, fitting it along the various lines on my hand. I opened my other palm and held my hands out to test if the balance between them was affected by the weight of the thread. It wasn't. I placed the thread on my tongue and let it rest there where its weight was more discernible. I half-expected a metallic taste of gold, but it tasted starchy like any other thread. Against the pores of my tongue, I could feel it growing thicker with the saliva that was gathering in my mouth. I swallowed both the saliva and the thread.

Immediately after, when it was already too late, it occurred to me that I had broken my fast.

It would be a mortal sin to receive the host, and yet the primary duty of a Knight was to march to the Communion rail leading the congregation. I sat trying to figure my way out of the predicament I'd created. I was feeling increasingly anxious, a little sick, actually, as if the thread had wound around my stomach. I knew that not one of my classmates would have even realized that they'd broken their fast by swallowing a thread, and since they wouldn't have realized it was a sin, then it wouldn't have been one. It didn't seem quite fair that my greater understanding made me more culpable. Perhaps, I thought, a thread doesn't count as food, but I knew I was grasping for excuses—it seemed a dubious distinction to risk one's soul upon. Communion was fast approaching and I grew increasingly upset, thinking up various plans at what seemed a feverish pace and rejecting them just as feverishly. I couldn't merely sit in my seat while the others filed up. Maybe I could pretend to be even sicker than I was feeling, or to faint, but the notion of lying during the Mass was too repellent and probably another mortal sin against the Eighth Commandment. I'd just be getting myself in deeper.

Then, I thought of a detail mentioned by Sister Aurelia before our First Holy Communion: how if one should ever realize at the communion rail that he has a mortal sin on his soul he'd somehow forgotten about until that moment, then rather than receive Communion, he was to merely clasp a hand in a *mea culpa* over his heart and bow his head, and the priest standing before him with the host would understand.

Communion time came and on shaky legs I marched to the rail with the other Knights. Father Pedro wearing his one-eyed pair of dark glasses approached, an altar boy at his elbow. I could hear his shoes on the carpet as he paused to deliver a host and move to the next Knight, I would hear him muttering the Latin prayer as he delivered each host to an awaiting tongue. *Corpus domini nostri Jesu Christi* . . . May the body of our Lord, Jesus Christ, preserve your soul in everlasting life.

Then he was before me and I clapped a fist against my heart and bowed my head. He stopped and peered down at me through the single lens of his glasses. He was trying to meet my eyes and having a hard time doing it with his single eye. Then, he regained his composure and moved on, wondering, I was sure, what grievous sin I had committed.

I never told him, nor anyone else. I had swallowed a thread. No one but God would ever know. It was my finest hour as a theologian. Only years later did I realize, it was the moment I would think back to when I'd come to wonder how I lost my faith.

SHEYENE FOSTER

# Storm Warnings

*When the peacock loudly bawls, soon we'll have both rain and squalls.*

At eight years old, I considered myself one of the top meteorologists in the county. I was intrigued by the mysterious, the unpredictable and unknown. On turbulent summer nights, I sat in our entryway on a wooden chair directly in front of the screen door, eyes angled heavenward, searching for some sign of disturbance. A brightening in the distant sky. A vague rumble of building thunder. The possibility of a tornado found in twisting gray clouds coiling upon themselves in the air, so much like the Lincoln Grade School lunch lady's permed silver hair.

As a storm built, so did my excitement, the thrill of unknown power in the air that could only be washed away with the rain. I delighted in each spark of lightning, every loud clap of thunder which would shake the entirety of our white bungalow. I was hooked. Mother finally gave up trying to dissuade me. I was always the stubborn child. She came over to the screen door with an accepting smile concealing slight impatience, and my dinner on a TV tray.

*The stronger the blast, the sooner 'tis past.*

Once the rain hit, I would go out on our porch, lean backwards over the railing, and let the cool raindrops saturate my stringy red hair to a dripping auburn. The moisture seeped into my skin, leaving it refreshed and alive. I thought it was a tremendous collaboration: Mother Earth and God shaking hands somewhere in the vast abyss. I wanted to harness their power, stretch my hands to the sky, and absorb their collective efforts.

Later, I learned it all has to do with atmosphere, the atmosphere of the earth, the atmosphere of our lives. Heating of the earth's land surface causes particles of warm air to rise to the level of condensation. If conditions are favorable, cumulus clouds then form mighty towers, and eventually merge into cumulonimbus clouds which may produce thunderstorms.

*Ringing in the ear indicates a change of wind.*

What is the folkloric indication for a simple change of heart? Tonight, in my mother's orange plaid kitchen, nothing I say can explain my defiance, my lack of faith in her God. I was *always* the stubborn child. Stubborn about little things— taking my cough syrup, coming indoors from outside play. Mother reacted with grudging patience. Tonight I have rejected her entire ideology, and she is furious beyond her usual thinly-veiled irritation. In the kitchen's harsh light, there is no place to hide. Through her tears, she reminds me of my once-stubborn determination to believe.

"Whatever happened to that little girl who helped me when Poppy died?" she questions. "The one who told me, 'Don't cry, Mommy. Everything will be all right because Poppy's in heaven with Jesus.'"

I have no answers. That little girl has been lost somewhere in the storm, whisked away by the winds of time. I am the woman who is left, wishing once again for a powerful thunderstorm. A surge of strength from the sky, loud thunder to block out my mother's question. The sky remains clear, however, and I stay silent. The only drops fall from Mother's eyes, salty and stained by black mascara, leaving wet, grayish trails down her cheeks.

*Cruel storms do not blow in a right course.*

JANE GUILBAULT

## This Is Your Day

It seems like my First Communion again, a day I recall with
clarity, not the events but the quality, the exact quality of sunlight, the color and smell of new grass, warmth, a white dress.
I suppose I remember it because it was rare to be singled out,
to be acknowledged apart from my sisters. After Mass, I would
ride down to Scranton, still in my dress, sit quietly in the living rooms of relatives to collect a five- or ten-dollar bill.

But I am not six. I am twenty-three and just married. Today
has that same quality—the day overbright, too warm for May,
the same little country church, the Endless Mountains extend-
ing around us. I feel the same confusion at being the center of
attention, the same vague sense of accomplishment. Other
than walk through a ceremony, I don't know what I have done
to win the approval of a hard-to-please extended family. I am

only pretending to be what I have never felt myself to be—
charming, friendly, attractive, a loving and grateful daughter.

We are drunk and sleepy, the inside of the car like a greenhouse. My husband drives. I am still in ivory organdy, my two
sisters in sapphire blue shantung. We are quiet for the first
time today, driving down to Scranton to see my eighty-nine-
year-old grandmother who is too frail to attend the wedding.
This is something I had not wanted to do, but the only thing
my mother insisted upon.

My grandmother is irritated with being left alone all day. "It's
about time," she yells when she hears us on the stairs, but her
face brightens when we sweep into her tiny room. I sit on the
bed in my big dress. She is sitting in a straight-backed armchair as she always does. We recount the small details of the
day, but it isn't enough to distract her from herself. "I tell ya
this is no way to live," she says.

This moment intrudes starkly upon a day unnaturally full of
joy—the reality that I wanted to avoid on my wedding day.
Throughout the planning stages I was stubborn; the bridal magazines say a modern bride should have things her way: *This is
your day,* they say, as if a woman gets only one day of autonomy.
I thought of my mother's life, one long timeline of sacrifice; she
went from living with her demanding parents to a career in nursing, to marriage and children, then back to nursing her elderly
parents. So I was determined to preserve some trace of myself.

At one point I tried on my mother's wedding dress with no
intention of wearing it. It is gorgeous, but not me, too fifties,
with high neck, cap sleeves, bouffant skirt. I wanted something
A-line, modern. My mother wouldn't say what she wanted, but

sat on the bed running her hand over the material. She was quiet and wistful that her dress hadn't been well-preserved, the color turned in spots, the veil missing rhinestones. "I loved this dress," she says. Another story is the going-away outfit she was made to wear after the wedding—a floral sheath, a gold coat with a pilgrim collar, a pilgrimlike hat.

My mother admonished, "You should go see your grandmother; she'll be dead soon," the common combination of death and threats. But within a year and a half of my wedding, both my mother and my grandmother were dead. *Now all the days are yours and yours alone.* Nana outlasted everyone with sheer force of will, whereas my mother's heart gave out with too much worry, her will like her favorite tree outside our dining room window, soft and spindly, branches bending and breaking every winter, a tropical thing transplanted to a harsher climate. Every year she would doubt her ability to make it through the winter. She died in December.

Candids, I instructed the photographer, wanting no phoniness. So there are no pictures of my mother helping me get ready, something we would never have done in real life. But in one of the frames, my mother, as if wishing it were so, turns and touches my veil.

In photos that catch me, she is just off-center, fragmented. In one, my sisters watch while I dance with my father. In the right third is my mother's round, freckled forearm, her hand holding a wadded-up handful of tissues. Is it possible that she was crying? If the photographer could have known what would happen, he might have panned to the right, brought her into focus. I might have turned to face the camera's white flash, wearing a different dress, the one my mother loved.

M. J. IUPPA

# The Weather of Distance

Beneath the willows' feathery boughs, a yellow-crowned night heron stands motionless at the pond's edge. The pond appears sullen, deep emerald, like an eye struck open to its insult. It waits and sees, in defiant countenance. Only the graceful current of a water strider streaks its glassy surface.

*

It's February, a year since my mother's diagnosis of cancer; she's no longer waiting. A cup of Irish Breakfast tea with a full teaspoon of raspberry honey takes the chill off the morning and soothes my raw throat. The rain and fog of three days keeps the distance of weather. I'm stuck in a dreary pattern.

*

Nothing heals. One minute becomes memory of Mother's dark brown eyes looking beyond conversations, while her hands skillfully slice fresh Red Haven peaches to put by for winter. There are three Zip-lock bags full in the freezer. The last harvest. I imagine eating these peaches slowly, letting the slippery, cold, orange slices melt down into her way of relish—something exceptional. It makes me feel rich.

*

All summer, tumbled glacier stones, stones which haven't been unearthed in years, are found in abundance on the lake shore. Stones no bigger than my fingertip, or large enough to fit in the cup of my hand. Somehow precious stones—red, green, yellow, blue, gray, and pink—the colors of my family's emotions. My sister prizes them. She hand picks them, organizes them in shape and size and color, spends hours wrapping each one in gold or silver wire. She's harnessing the earth's energy. She's keeping my mother alive.

*

Not one family of ruby-throated hummingbirds, but three. All cunning and warring for the red liquid in the feeder at the kitchen window. Always wanting more. So much like us.

*

Driving home from a swim meet with my daughter Meaghan, I notice she's pensive, wet-haired, hungry. She's looking out the window, up into the darkening winter sky; watching the rising full moon. It's been five full moons since the night my mother died. She says, "I can't remember Grandma's voice. Make her voice for me." I look at her silhouette, her patience with me as I say her name, "May-gan May-gan," the way my mother would sing it. She smiles. "It's coming back."

JAMES SALTER

# The Brilliance

How well one remembers that world, the whiff of jet exhaust, oily and dark, in the morning air as you walk to where the planes are parked out in the mist.

Soon you are up near the sun where the air is burning cold, amid all that is familiar, the scratches on the canopy, the chipped black of the instrument panel, the worn red cloth of the safety streamers stuffed in a pocket down near your shoe. From the tailpipe of the leader's plane comes an occasional dash of smoke, the only sign of motion as it streaks rearwards.

Below, the earth has shed its darkness. There is the silver of countless lakes and streams. The greatest things to be seen, the ancients wrote, are sun, stars, water, and clouds. Here among them, of what is one thinking? I cannot remember but probably of nothing, of flying itself, the imperishability of it, the brilliance. You do not think about the fish in the great,

winding river, thin as string, miles below, or the frogs in the
glinting ponds, nor they of you; they know little of you,
though once, just after takeoff, I saw the shadow of my plane
skimming the dry grass like the wings of god and passing over,
frozen by the noise, a hare two hundred feet below. That lone
hare, I, the morning sun, and all that lay beyond it were for an
instant joined, like an eclipse.

One night in early spring there were two of us—I was
wingman. No one else was flying at the time. We were landing
in a formation after an instrument approach. It was very dark,
it had been raining, and the leader misread the threshold lights.
We crossed the end of the runway high and touched down
long. In exact imitation I held the nose high, as he did, to slow
down, wheels skipping along the concrete like flat stones on a
lake. Halfway down we lowered the noses and started to brake.
Incredibly we began to go faster. The runway, invisible and
black, was covered with the thinnest sheet of ice. Light rain
had frozen sometime after sundown and the tower did not
know it. We might, at the last moment, have gone around—
put on full power and tried to get off again—but it was too
close. We were braking in desperation. I stop-cocked my
engine—shut it off to provide greater air resistance—and a
moment later he called that he was doing the same. We were
standing on the brakes and then releasing, hard on and off.
The end of the runway was near. The planes were slithering,
skidding sideways. I knew we were going off and that we might
collide. I had full right rudder in, trying to stay to the side.

We slid off the end of the runway together and went
about two hundred feet on the broken earth before we finally
stopped. Just ahead of us was the perimeter road and beyond
it, lower, some railroad tracks.

When I climbed out of the cockpit I wasn't shaking. I felt
almost elated. It could have been so much worse. The duty

officer came driving up. He looked at the massive, dark shapes of the planes, awkwardly placed near each other, the long empty highway behind them, the embankment ahead. "Close one, eh?" he said.

This was at Fürstenfeldbruck, the most lavish of the pre-war German airfields, near Munich. We came there from our own field, Bitburg, in the north, the Rhineland, to stand alert or fire gunnery close by. Zulu alert, two ships on five-minute, two on fifteen. The long well-built barracks, the red tile roofs and marble corridors. The stands of pine on the way to the pilots' dining room, where you could eat breakfast in your flying suit and the waitresses knew what you preferred.

Munich was our city, its great night presence, the bars and clubs, the Isar green and pouring like a faucet through its banks, the Regina Hotel, dancing on Sunday afternoons, faces damp with the heat, the Film Casino Bar, Bei Heinz. All the women, Panas's girlfriend in the low-cut dress, Van Bockel's, who was a secretary and had such an exceptional figure, Cortada's, who smelled like a florist's on a warm day. Munich in the snow, coming back to the field alone on the streetcar.

I flew back to Bitburg with White, one of the two men in the squadron to become famous—Aldrin was the other—on a winter day. It was late in the afternoon, everything blue as metal, the sky, the towns and forests, even the snow. The other ship, silent, constant on your wing. With the happiness of being with someone you like, through it we went together, at thirty-five thousand, the thin froth of contrails fading behind.

White had been the first person I met when I came to the squadron and I knew him well. In the housing area he and his wife lived on our stairway. He had a fair, almost milky, complexion and reddish hair. An athlete, a hurdler; you see his face on many campuses, idealistic, aglow. He was an excellent pilot, acknowledged as such by those implacable judges, the ground crews. They did not revere him as they did the ruffians who might drink with them, discuss the merits of the squadron commander or sexual exploits, but they respected him and his proper, almost studious, ways. God and country—these were the things he had been bred for.

In Paris, a lifetime later, in a hotel room I watched as on screens everywhere he walked dreamily in space, the first American to do so. I was nervous and depressed. My chest ached. My hair had patches of gray. White was turning slowly, upside down, tethered to the spacecraft by a lazy cord. I was sick with envy—he was destroying hope. Whatever I might do, it would not be as overwhelming as this. I felt a kind of loneliness and terror. I wanted to be home, to see my children again before the end, and I was certain it was near the end; I felt suicidal, ready to burst into tears. He did this to me unknowingly, as a beautiful woman crossing the street crushes hearts beneath her heel.

White burned to ashes in the terrible accident on the launching pad at Cape Canaveral in 1967. He died with Virgil Grissom, with whom I had also flown. His funeral was solemn. I attended, feeling out of place. To be killed flying had always been a possibility, but the two of them had somehow moved beyond that. They were already visible in that great photograph of our time, the one called celebrity. Still youthful and, so far as I knew, unspoiled, they were like jockeys moving to the post for an event that would mark the century, the race to the moon. The absolutely unforeseen destroyed them. Aldrin went instead.

White is buried in the same cemetery as my father, not far away. I visit both graves when I am there. White's, though amid others, seems visible from some distance off, just as he himself was if you looked intently at the ranks.

JOSEPHINE JACOBSEN

# Artifacts of Memory

Archeology, the dictionary says, is "the study of material remains of past human life and activities." More than that, it is the seedbed of memory, and its fascination comes from the leap we take into continuity.

Trudging the sunbaked streets of Pompeii, bombarded by the guide's dramatic inaccuracies, what we really look at, look for, are resemblances with familiar things: this atrium where guests gathered, noisily conversational; that room where hungry and thirsty people ate fruit and drank wine. We know that when the hot ashes fell, people were selling and buying; taking a nap; bathing; worrying; arranging flowers; making love.

The knowledge is partly a tiny chill, partly a warmth of recognition. It is like a hand touching our shoulder. What we are really concerned with is not the dead, but the living: those people, then; us, now.

Theirs was a sophisticated generation, concerned with many of the things that concern us. But going back into time, our archeologist brings up to the sun traces of an age buried profoundly in the past. It is, as a book title tersely put it, *The Testimony of the Spade.* And again we feel, this time more strangely, the combined chill and warmth: this woman prepared food for her children; that man built a fire for protection and warmth; when night fell, they wanted fire and shelter and human company.

Art was imitation and magic; but something else, too. In the caves of Lascaux the innermost and highest paintings were too high to have been visible by any illumination then possessed; the artist was not painting for the observer. In the dizzying tables of centuries, how very close they are to us, the vanguard of a beleaguered and recent army of human beings.

Archeology has a way of slipping out of its technical boundaries—it haunts all aspects of memory. Planting a garden, on an early June morning, I unearth a rubber soldier; and that tiny object, grubby, one-legged, re-creates instantly a June a quarter of a century gone by, the heat, the flowers, the voice, the gesture. Was the rubber man buried by accident, or with ceremony? Like any vessel, or trinket, or tool, it speaks of its owner, demands our recognition.

It is the same with a blackened chimney, strangled by wild roses, with no house to warm. We are stopped suddenly by the hieroglyph, which will tell us nothing except that someone passed here and paused, for years or decades, a message we will never translate more accurately, but cannot fail to understand.

The fascination of ghost stories is the fascination of archeology. Ghosts are revenants, they revisit the glimpses of the moon. Who were you? we ask. Did you live here? What happened to you? What do you want? There are, so to speak, implicit as well as explicit ghosts. Standing in the great square of Monte Alban in quiet sunlight, the visitor finds it enigmatically peopled, crowded with its own life, priests, warriors, victims. The ball court, where to lose the game was to lose life, vibrates with its players.

Psychiatrists are archeologists. Who are you? they ask. What happened to you? Let us excavate that minute, that incident, that morning twenty years ago, that childhood night.

We are ourselves archeologists. Come back in early May to a house shut up through a mountain winter. The time lapse is not centuries, but months. Yet it is the past we explore as surely as though it were six centuries. It is, indeed, the past. In the wastebasket is the stub of a ticket for the barn theatre, whose actors, like their audience of that summer night, are elsewhere. The calendar on the kitchen wall is for an October gone with its leaves. In the porch rafters, a sluttish bunch of twigs held eggs, now wings, and on the big lilac bush by the door, brown lumps are the traces of purple cones that drew hordes of monarch butterflies, come three thousand miles from a Mexico winter, to wave and fan in the heat. In the attic playroom, burly logs are ashes in the chunk stove; a broken crayon drew something unpreserved. It is a rare house that will have no trace of someone who will not come back.

Making us human, layer on layer the artifacts of memory lie. The pharaohs, all the emperors who designed tombs of magnificence, simply say together: Remember me. Layer on layer, the cities lie. In the mind, layer on layer of memory. In the house, summer on summer, its hours and minutes. From the men of Lascaux to last year's June, the distance is short.

# Biographical Notes

RICK BASS is a petroleum geologist and environmental activist and the author of twelve books of fiction and nonfiction. Among his most recent books are *The New Wolves*, *The Book of Yaak* (a plea for saving the Yaak Valley), *The Sky, The Stars, The Wilderness*, and the novel *Where the Sea Used to Be*. He lives with his family in northern Montana.

CHARLES BAXTER is the author of six books of fiction, most recently *Believers* (Pantheon). He is also the author of a book of essays published by Graywolf, *Burning Down the House*. He has received grants from The Guggenheim Foundation, the Lila Wallace–Reader's Digest Foundation, and the National Endowment for the Arts. He lives in Ann Arbor and teaches at the University of Michigan.

JANICE BEST is editor of *Elan*, and a senior at Douglas Anderson School of the Arts. A poet and painter, Best hopes to attend Florida State University as a creative writing major. She currently lives a bike-ride away from the St. Johns River in eastern Florida and works in a bookstore.

MARY CLEARMAN BLEW is the author of memoirs, *All But the Waltz* and *Balsamroot,* and two collections of short stories, *Lambing Out* and *Runaway.* She is the co-editor of *Circle of Women: An Anthology of Contemporary Western Women Writers.* She teaches at the University of Idaho.

MICHAEL BLUMENTHAL's collection of essays from Central Europe, *When History Enters the House,* was published by Pleasure Boat Studios in 1998. The author of five volumes of poetry and the novel *Weinstock Among the Dying* (winner of *Hadassah Magazine's* 1994 Harold Ribelow Prize), his sixth book of poems, *Dusty Angel,* will be published by BOA Editions. He presently lives and works in Austin, Texas.

JANE BROX is the author of *Five Thousand Days Like This One* (Beacon Press, 1999) and *Here and Nowhere Else,* which won the L. L. Winship/PEN New England Award. Her work has appeared in *Best American Essays* and numerous journals and magazines, including *The Georgia Review, The Gettysburg Review, Orion,* and *New England Review.* She lives in the Merrimack Valley of Massachusetts.

KATHLEEN CAIN is the author of *Luna: Myth and Mystery,* a book about the role of the moon in human history. She is a contributing editor for *Bloomsbury Review* and a recipient of a literature fellowship from the Colorado Council on the Arts and Humanities. She lives in Arvada, Colorado, and is coordinator of library instruction at Front Range Community College.

ANNE CARSON won the 1996 Lannan Prize for Poetry. She was born in Canada and teaches ancient Greek for a living. She has published books of poetry, a memoir, and a "novel in verse" entitled *Autobiography of Red.* Otherwise, she spends most of her time painting volcanoes.

BERNARD COOPER is the author of *Maps to Anywhere* (University of Georgia Press) and, most recently, a collection of memoirs entitled *Truth Serum* (Houghton Mifflin). He is the recipient of the 1991 PEN/USA Ernest Hemingway Award and a 1995 O. Henry Prize. His work has appeared in *Best American Essays* of 1995, 1997, and 1998; and in such magazines and literary reviews as *Harper's, Paris Review,* and the *Los Angeles Times Magazine.*

KELLY CUNNANE's creative nonfiction can be found in *Stet, Sojourner*, and *Grand Tour*. Her illustrations are included in *Intricate Weave* (Iris Editions) and in her award-winning metajournal "Come Out on the Daylight," found in *The Gamut* (CSU). Heinemann International distributes her children's books to readers in Africa. She lives downeast on an island with her husband and four children; she is currently working on a novel based on her experiences in Alaska.

EDWIDGE DANTICAT was born in Haiti and is the author of *Breath, Eyes, Memory* (Soho Press, 1995), chosen by the Oprah Book Club, and a collection of short stories *krik? krak!* (Soho Press, 1995), a nominee for the National Book Award. Her most recent book is *The Farming of Bones* (Soho Press, 1998), about the 1937 massacre of Haitians at the border of the Dominican Republic.

TENAYA DARLINGTON lives in Madison, Wisconsin. Her work has appeared in *Harper's Ferry, Mid-American Review, Sonora Review*, and Scribner's *Best of the Fiction Workshops for 1998*, among others. She is currently the writing fellow at Beloit College.

ANN DAUM lives in the White River Valley of western South Dakota. She now shares the family ranch with five cats, nineteen horses, and five hundred (or so) mother cows. When she's not in the barn, she's working on her first book, a collection of personal essays.

SEAMUS DEANE is a native of Ireland. He is the author of a number of books of criticism and poetry, as well as the novel *Reading in the Dark* (Knopf, 1997). He teaches at the University of Notre Dame.

HARRIET DOERR is a native of Pasadena, California, and was awarded the Stegner Fellowship at Stanford. Her books include *Stones for Ibarra* and *Consider This, Señora*. Among her awards are the American Book Award, PEN Award for Fiction, NEA Fellowship, and American Academy and Institute of Arts and Letters. She is working on recollections in story form.

ARIEL DORFMAN is a Chilean expatriate who lives with his family in Durham, North Carolina, where he holds the Walter Hines Page chair at Duke University. He writes poems, stories, novels, plays, essays, and recently a memoir. His many titles include *Konfidenz, Mascara,* and *Death and the Maiden.*

BRIAN DOYLE is the editor of *Portland Magazine* at the University of Portland, Oregon. His essays and poems have appeared in *Atlantic Monthly, American Scholar, Orion,* and *Commonweal,* among other publications. He and his father, Jim Doyle, are the authors of *Two Voices* (1996), a collection of their essays. His essays, *Credo,* will be published by Liguori in 1999.

ANDRE DUBUS is the author of nine works of fiction as well as books of essays, the most recent of which is *Meditations from a Movable Chair.* He received the PEN/Malamud Award, the *Boston Globe*'s first Lawrence L. Winship Award, and fellowships both from the Guggenheim and from the MacArthur Foundations. He died in 1999.

STUART DYBEK is the author of *Brass Knuckles,* a collection of poems, two collections of stories, *Childhood and Other Neighborhoods* and *The Coast of Chicago,* as well as a chapbook of short shorts, *The Story of Mist.* His essays have appeared in anthologies such as *Family* and *Townships.* "Thread" is from a sequence of essays titled "St. Stuart."

JOHN EDWARDS is a writer and prison-reform activist. He is the author of *Prison Man Learns Things,* a nonfiction book about the criminal justice system in which "Prison Man Considers Turkey" will be included. The essay won a 1997 National Public Radio writing competition and was broadcast on *Weekend Edition.* With Diana Hume George, Edwards reviews films and is completing a nonfiction book entitled *Coming Clean: Grim Truths about Sex.*

SHEYENE FOSTER is a sophomore at Kansas State University. This is her first publication, taken from *Nebraska Review.*

CASTLE FREEMAN, JR. is the author of short stories, novels, and essays. His collection of essays, *Spring Snow* (Houghton Mifflin, 1995), is a series of short pieces written for the *Old Timer's Almanac.* His most recent novel (University Presses of New England) is titled *Judgment Hill.* He lives in southern Vermont.

CELINE GEARY claims to have no "bio." She is a mother during the day and takes several classes every semester at night—bio enough.

KINERETH GENSLER is the author of *Journey Fruit*, a collection of poems and a memoir, and two books of poems, as well as co-author of a textbook, *The Poetry Connection: An Anthology of Contemporary Poems with Ideas to Stimulate Children's Writing*. She has been a Fellow at MacDowell and Ragdale. She teaches in the Radcliffe Seminars in Cambridge, Massachusetts.

DIANA HUME GEORGE is the author of *The Lonely Other: A Woman Watching America* and a number of books of poetry and literary criticism, including *Oedipus Anne: The Poetry of Anne Sexton*, *The Resurrection of the Body*, and *A Genesis*. With Constance Coiner, she edited *The Family Track*. George teaches creative writing at the Pennsylvania State University at Erie. She is editing or co-authoring nonfiction books with Sonya Jones and with John Edwards.

CECILE GODING is from Florence, South Carolina, where she coordinated neighborhood literacy projects for some years. She is a graduate student in the University of Iowa's program in nonfiction writing and the Iowa Writers' Workshop. Her poetry chapbook, *The Women Who Drink at the Sea*, was published by State Street Press.

ALBERT GOLDBARTH's essays have been collected in two books, *A Sympathy of Souls* and *Great Topics of the World*, and have appeared in *Best American Essays*, *The Best American Movie Writing*, the *Pushcart* anthology, and elsewhere. He is also the author of numerous books of poetry, including *Heaven and Earth*, winner of the National Book Critics Circle Award.

KIMBERLY GORALL is an activist, a full-time technical writer, and a part-time graduate student in upstate New York. "The End of Summer" is her first appearance in print.

VIVIAN GORNICK has been a staff writer for the *Village Voice* and contributes regularly to the *New York Times* and other journals. Her books include her memoir, *Fierce Attachments*, plus *Women in Science: Portraits from a World in Transition* and *Approaching Eye Level*. Her awards include a Guggenheim Fellowship and a grant from the Ford Foundation. She lives in New York City.

JEANNE BRINKMAN GRINNAN coordinates and teaches in the first-year writing program at SUNY Brockport. She lives in Rochester, New York, and is working on a series of essays remembering her father. "Adjustments" is one of them.

JANE GUILBAULT has an MA from SUNY Brockport, where she teaches freshman composition. She writes poetry and essays, two of which recently appeared in *The Gettysburg Review*.

PATRICIA HAMPL is a poet, anthologist, and memoirist. *Virgin Time: In Search of the Contemplative Life* was reissued by Ballantine in 1998, and her award-winning *A Romantic Education* was reissued by W. W. Norton. In addition, Norton published her book on imagination and memory, entitled *I Could Tell You Stories* (1999). She is the recipient of many awards, including a MacArthur Fellowship.

DERMOT HEALY is an Irish novelist, poet, and playwright. His books include the award-winning novel *A Goat's Song*, as well as *The Bend for Home*, a memoir. He lives in Sligo, Ireland.

STEVE HELLER is the author of many published works of fiction, including a collection of short stories, *The Man Who Drank a Thousand Beers*, and an award-winning novel, *The Automotive History of Lucky Kellerman*. He recently began writing nonfiction and has new essays in *Manoa, Flint Hills Literary Review, Hawai'i Review*, and elsewhere. He chairs the creative writing program at Kansas State University.

R. H. HERZOG has published short stories and essays in magazines and journals. He teaches composition and literature at Monroe Community College in Rochester, New York. Currently he is working on two books, one a historical narrative based on family correspondence dating from the mid-nineteenth century, and the second a novel of a bizarre community college professor (which may be more autobiographical than he intended).

WILLIAM HEYEN teaches at SUNY Brockport, where he is Poet in Residence. He is the author of *With Me Far Away*, a memoir of his

Long Island boyhood. His books of poetry include *Erika: Poems of the Holocaust*, *Pterodactyl Rose: Poems of Ecology*, and *Crazy Horse in Stillness*, which won the 1997 Small Press Books Award. *Pig Notes & Dumb Music: Prose on Poetry* and *Diana, Charles, and the Queen: Poems* appeared from BOA Editions in 1998.

M . J . I U P P A  is the author of *Sometimes Simply*, a chapbook of poetry published by Foreseeable Future Press. Her poems have appeared in *Yankee, Poetry, Tar River Poetry*, and other literary journals. She teaches creative writing workshops through Young Audiences, Genesee Valley BOCES, Project U.N.I.Q.U.E., Writers & Books literary center, and is a part-time faculty member at St. John Fisher College in Rochester, New York. She lives on a small farm near Lake Ontario.

J O S E P H I N E   J A C O B S E N 's recent books are *In the Crevice of Time* (poetry, Hopkins, 1995), *What Goes Without Saying* (fiction, Hopkins, 1996), and *The Instant of Knowing* (nonfiction, Michigan, 1997). She is a member of the American Academy of Arts and Letters and a recipient of the Robert Frost Medal for Lifetime Achievement from the Poetry Society of America. She lives in Baltimore, Maryland.

J A M E S   K I L G O  teaches at the University of Georgia. His books include *Deep Enough for Ivorybills* and *Inheritance of Horses*. His essays have appeared in such publications as *The Georgia Review, The Gettysburg Review*, and *Sewanee Review*.

J A M A I C A   K I N C A I D 's most recent nonfiction is a memoir about her brother's death, *My Brother*. She is also the author of *The Autobiography of My Mother*, as well as many books of fiction. She lives and gardens in southern Vermont.

V E R L Y N   K L I N K E N B O R G  is the author of *Making Hay* and *The Last Fine Time*. He is the recipient of an NEA Fellowship and a Lila Wallace–Reader's Digest Writer's Award. He is currently a member of the editorial board of the *New York Times* and lives in upstate New York.

W I L L I A M   K L O E F K O R N  lives and writes in Lincoln, Nebraska. His books of poetry include *Dragging Sand Creek for Minnows*, *Covenants* (with Utah poet David Lee), *Houses and Beyond*, and

*Treehouse: New & Selected Poems.* His memoir, *This Death by Drowning,* appeared in 1997 from the University of Nebraska Press.

YUSEF KOMUNYAKAA is Professor of Creative Writing at Princeton University. His book of poetry, *Noon Vernacular,* won the Pulitzer Prize and the Kingsley–Tufts Poetry Award from the Claremont Graduate School.

GUY LEBEDA is a journalist, essayist, and photographer who writes about art, the environment, and outdoor topics. His work has appeared in *Tallahassee Magazine, Capital City, Valley Horse Journal, Salt Lake City Magazine,* and others. His comedy radio script was performed by Garrison Keillor on National Public Radio. He is the Literature Program Coordinator for the Utah Arts Council.

DAWN MARANO is an acquisitions editor at the University of Utah Press. Her poetry and nonfiction appear in the anthology *The Sacred Place* and in *When We Say We're Home,* forthcoming from the University of Utah Press. "Fallout" is excerpted from "The Half of It," which originally appeared in *Ascent* and was cited as a Notable Essay of 1996 in *Best American Essays.*

DIONISIO D. MARTÍNEZ, born in Cuba, is the author of three poetry collections, including *Bad Alchemy* (Norton, 1995). A recipient of fellowships from the Guggenheim Foundation, the National Endowment for the Arts, and the Whiting Foundation, he lives in Tampa, Florida. His reviews and essays appear in the *Miami Herald,* the *Atlanta Journal-Constitution,* and elsewhere.

WILLIAM MAXWELL was born in Lincoln, Illinois, in 1908. His books include *Bright Center of Heaven; They Came Like Swallows; So Long, See You Tomorrow;* and *All the Days and Nights.* Recipient of the National Book Award, he has also been awarded the PEN/Malamud Award and the Howells Medal of the American Academy of Arts and Letters. He lives with his wife in New York City.

REBECCA McCLANAHAN is the author of three books of poetry (most recently, *The Intersection of X and Y* from Copper Beech Press), a book of lectures and readings (*One Word Deep)* and *Word Painting:*

*Writing More Descriptively* (Story Press). She has received a Pushcart Prize, the Wood Prize for Poetry, and the Carter prize for nonfiction from *Shenandoah*. Her essays have appeared in *The Gettysburg Review, Southern Review, Kenyon Review, The Creative Nonfiction Reader*, and elsewhere.

FRANK MCCOURT was for many years a writing teacher at Stuyvesant High School in New York City and performed with his brother Malachy in *A Couple of Blaguards*, a musical review about their Irish youth. His memoir, *Angela's Ashes*, won the National Book Critics Circle Award, The *Los Angeles Times* Book Award, and the Pulitzer Prize. He lives in New York City and is at work on a new memoir.

JOHN MCPHEE is perhaps America's best-known writer of nonfiction. His books include *Coming into the Country, Assembling California, The Control of Nature, Rising from the Plains, The Pine Barrens, The Headmaster,* and more than a dozen other titles, including the recent compilation of his geology books, *Annals of a Former World*, and two volumes of *The John McPhee Reader*. He lives and works in Princeton, New Jersey.

JAMES ALAN MCPHERSON has recently published two books, *Crabcakes* and *Fathering Daughters* (co-edited with Dewitt Henry). He is currently a Fellow in the Center for Advanced Study in the Behavioral Sciences at Stanford University. He teaches regularly at the University of Iowa. His work has appeared in *Best American Short Stories, Best American Essays*, and *O. Henry Prize Stories*. McPherson has received a Guggenheim Fellowship and a MacArthur Prize Fellows Award.

BRENDA MILLER's collection of essays, *A Thousand Buddhas*, recently won first place in the Utah Arts Council Original Writing Competition. She received a Pushcart Prize for an essay that originally appeared in *The Georgia Review*, and her work has appeared or is forthcoming in *Prairie Schooner, Northern Lights, Seattle Magazine*, and elsewhere. Her essay "A Thousand Buddhas" is reprinted in *Storming Heaven's Gate: An Anthology of Spiritual Writings by Women*. She is the nonfiction editor of *Quarterly West*.

N. SCOTT MOMADAY is a poet, novelist, playwright, and artist. He won the Pulitzer Prize for fiction for *House Made of Dawn*. His books also include *The Way to Rainy Mountain, The Names, The Ancient Child, In the Presence of the Sun, The Man Made of Words,* and *In the Bear's House.* He is a member of the American Academy of Arts and Sciences and the Iowa Tribe Gourd Dance Society. He lives in New Mexico.

KATHLEEN DEAN MOORE's collection of essays, *Riverwalking: Reflections on Moving Water*, won the 1996 Pacific Northwest Booksellers' Award. Her creative nonfiction appears in the *New York Times Magazine,* the *North American Review, Field and Stream,* and elsewhere. The chair of the Philosophy Department at Oregon State University, Moore is the author also of three philosophical books, including a study of the president's pardoning power.

KATHLEEN NORRIS's most recent book is *Amazing Grace: A Vocabulary of Faith* (Riverhead, 1998). She is also the author of *The Cloister Walk* (Riverhead, 1996) and *Dakota,* which won the 1993 Quality Paperback's New Visions Award. She lives in northwestern South Dakota on her grandparents' family farm and has received grants from the Guggenheim and Bush Foundations.

ROBERT O'CONNOR is the author of the novel *Buffalo Soldiers* (Vintage Contemporaries, 1994). For five years he taught at a maximum-security prison in upstate New York, the basis of his forthcoming book, *Lifesaving.* In 1996, *Granta* magazine named him to its list of Best Young American Novelists. He teaches literature and creative writing at the State University of New York, College at Oswego.

MARY OLIVER, a recipient of the Pulitzer Prize and National Book Award, is the author of eight books of poetry, essays on poetry and writing, and a collection of essays, *Blue Pastures.* She teaches at Bennington College in Vermont.

W. SCOTT OLSEN is an associate professor of English and chair of the Environmental Studies program at Concordia College in Moorhead, Minnesota. His books include a collection of short stories, two books of nonfiction, and a textbook. With Scott Cairns, he edited an anthology, *The Sacred Place*. His most recent project is *When We Say We're Home*, a quartet about place.

CYNTHIA OZICK is the author of novels, essays, short stories, and a play. *Fame & Folly*, her most recent collection of essays, won the 1997 PEN–Spiegel–Diamonstein Award for the Art of the Essay. *The Puttermesser Papers*, a novel, was nominated for the 1998 National Book Award. She served as guest editor of *Best American Essays 1998*.

ANNE PANNING is the author of *The Price of Eggs*, a collection of short stories, and has published short fiction and creative nonfiction in journals such as *Black Warrior Review, South Dakota Review, Ambergris*, and *Writing for Our Lives*. She teaches at SUNY Brockport, and is currently working on a novel, *Carrot Lake, Carrot Cake*.

JOHN T. PRICE lives in Council Bluffs, Iowa, and teaches at the University of Nebraska–Omaha. His essays have appeared in the *Christian Science Monitor, Florida Review, North Dakota Quarterly*, and *Creative Nonfiction*.

JONATHAN RABAN's books include *Old Glory, Foreign Land, For Love and Money, Coasting*, and *Hunting Mister Heartbreak*. He won the W. H. Heinemann Award for Literature in 1982 and the Thomas Cook Award in 1981 and 1991. *Bad Land: An American Romance* won the National Book Critics Circle Award and was nominated as a *New York Times* Editors' Choice for Book of the Year. He has also edited *The Oxford Book of the Sea*. He lives in Seattle.

PATTIANN ROGERS's book-length essay, *The Dream of the Marsh Wren*, appeared in the Credo Series published by Milkweed Editions, spring 1999. *A Covenant of Seasons*, in collaboration with artist Joellyn Duesberry, was published by Hudson Hills Press in 1998. Her seventh book of poems, *Eating Bread and Honey*, was published by Milkweed Editions in 1997. She has received two NEA grants, a Guggenheim Fellowship, and a Poetry Fellowship from the Lannan Foundation.

JOHN ROSENTHAL is a photographer/essayist whose book of photographs, *Regarding Manhattan*, was published in the fall of 1997. Rosenthal's essays have appeared in *Five Points, The Sun: A Bell Ringing in the Empty Sky*, and many other publications. Rosenthal is also a commentator on NPR's *All Things Considered* and a guest lecturer at Duke University's Institute of the Arts.

JAMES SALTER is the author of *A Sport and a Pastime* (now in a Modern Library edition), *Light Years, The Hunters, Solo Faces, Dusk and Other Stories*, which won the PEN/Faulkner Award in 1988, and a memoir, *Burning the Days: Recollections*. He lives in Colorado and Long Island.

MARJORIE SANDOR is the author of a collection of stories, *A Night of Music*. Her short fiction has appeared in such anthologies as *Best American Short Stories, 1985* and *1988, Twenty Under Thirty, The Pushcart Prize XIII*. Her essays have appeared in *The Gift of Trout* (The Lyons Press), the *New York Times Magazine, The Georgia Review*, and elsewhere. A collection of essays, *The Night Gardener*, is forthcoming from the Lyons Press. She teaches at Oregon State University.

REG SANER's *Reaching Keet Seel: Ruin's Echo and the Anasazi* features the terrain and prehistoric cultures of the Southwest. His previous book, *The Four-Cornered Falcon: Essays on the Interior West*, won the Colorado Center for the Book Award in nonfiction, and with his several prize-winning books of poetry earned him the Wallace Stegner Award, conferred by the Center of the American West. He teaches at the University of Colorado, Boulder.

ROBERT SHAPARD has won an NEA Fellowship as well as a CLMP writing award; his nonfiction has appeared in *Cosmopolitan*, his fiction in the *New England Review* and *Dallas Morning News* Sunday magazine. He directs the creative writing program at the University of Hawaii, where he co-founded *Manoa: A Pacific Journal of International Writing* and co-edits the *Sudden Fiction* anthology series.

DAVID SHIELDS is the author of *Remote* (Knopf), a work of autobiographical nonfiction; *A Handbook for Drowning*, a collection of linked stories; and two novels, *Dead Language* and *Heroes*. His stories and essays have appeared in the *New York Times Magazine, Harper's, Vogue, Village Voice, Details*, and *Utne Reader*.

KELLY SIMON's work has appeared in *The Quarterly, Ploughshares, Ellery Queen Magazine, Traveler's Tales* (Hong Kong, Food, and Italy), and elsewhere. *Alaska Quarterly* will publish vignettes from her memoir in progress. She is the recipient of the 1998 Lowell Thomas Award, and Weldon Press has published her Thai cookbook.

ANNICK SMITH is the author of *Homestead,* a memoir (Milkweed, 1998), and *Big Bluestem, Journey into the Tallgrass,* published by Council Oak Books and The Nature Conservancy. Her essays and stories have appeared in *Story, Audubon, Best American Short Stories,* and other anthologies. Smith was executive producer of the prize-winning film *Heartland* and a co-producer of *A River Runs Through It.* She lives on a homestead ranch in western Montana.

BRADY UDALL has published short stories in *GQ, Paris Review, Playboy,* and *Story.* His short-story collection, *Letting Loose the Hounds,* originally published by W. W. Norton, is now out in paperback from Washington Square Press. He recently moved from Idaho to Pennsylvania, where he teaches at Franklin and Marshall College, and is at work on a novel. His essay in this collection first appeared in *Personals: dreams and nightmares from the lives of 20 young writers.*

PAUL WEST has published seventeen novels and a dozen books of nonfiction. His most recent novels are *Terrestrials* and *Life with Swan.* His honors include the Literature Award from the American Academy of Arts and Letters and the Lannan Prize for Fiction. The government of France recently made him a Chevalier of Arts and Letters. His next nonfiction book (essays) will be the fourth volume of *Sheer Fiction.*

# Permissions